AIRCRAFT
AIRCRAFT

AIRCRAFT
AIRCRAFT

JOHN W. R. TAYLOR

HAMLYN
LONDON / NEW YORK / SYDNEY / TORONTO

CONTENTS

Designed by Keith Davis
Published by
THE HAMLYN PUBLISHING GROUP LTD
LONDON – NEW YORK – SYDNEY – TORONTO
Hamlyn House – Feltham –
Middlesex – England
First edition 1967
Revised edition 1970
© Copyright The Hamlyn Publishing Group Ltd 1967
ISBN 0 600 00037 0
Printed in Italy by Arnoldo Mondadori Editore - Verona

Title page illustration: Red Arrows formation team in action
(MoD-RAF photograph, Crown Copyright reserved)

ABOUT THIS BOOK

This, I hope, is an aviation history with a difference. The important dates, facts and figures that one expects to find in such a book are here, but an attempt has been made to put them into fresh perspective. It is all too easy for the historian to record that, for example, the Wrights were first to fly a powered aeroplane, or that the Heinkel He 178 was the first jet-plane, and leave it at that. But is there any particular merit in being first with something that is a dead end? Surely the true greatness of the Wrights lay in what they achieved later, not in those first shaky hops in December 1903 for which they are chiefly honoured?

Every fact in this book is founded on the very latest research, particularly that of my friend Charles Gibbs-Smith, who has done more than any man living to correct long-cherished fallacies and give due prominence to the work of true pioneers like Sir George Cayley. Some persistent errors in recorded history are corrected for the first time, such as the identity of the first jet-fighter used in action in World War 2.

I hope that the illustrations also will strike a new and welcome note. There seemed little point in presenting once more the same old prints of certain historical machines simply because they are the only contemporary pictures available. Use is made of photographs of authentic models belonging to the famous Qantas collection — giving a completely new impression of what Cayley's boy-carrier and Leonardo's man-powered machine were really like. The lightness of parts of the text is complemented by beautifully drawn cartoons from the BP film *Power to Fly.*

Biggest difference of all between this aviation history and others is that the reader is faced repeatedly with the question 'Is this the kind of flying about which the pioneers dreamed for so many years? In fact, is it flying at all?' The answer may be that only the amateur in his ultra-light home-built aeroplane and the glider pilot really know what it is to fly.

J. W. R. T.

BLAME THE BIRDS!

Very few people fly.

Such a statement may seem ridiculous at a time when nearly one million people travel by scheduled airline services every day, when an airliner takes off somewhere in the world every three seconds of the day and night, and when passenger-carrying airliners fly nearly 5,000 million miles each year—equivalent to 200,000 times round the world or 10,000 return trips to the Moon. But do airline passengers really fly?

The men who first thought about flying and dreamed of wheeling gracefully through the air, like birds, would admire the technical achievements of modern aviation; but they would hardly feel that it fulfilled their ambition. A journey by air is a rather dull and commonplace hop from one place to another. It is faster than rail, road or sea travel, but little more adventurous. This is what the average passenger wants. He is quite happy to leave the sensation of real flying to those who like that kind of thing. He would not wish to exchange his armchair seat, in an air-conditioned cabin, for the draughty thrills of an open cockpit; and he is quite content to entrust the piloting to somebody up front, who he knows only as a disembodied voice that bids him welcome over the aircraft's public address system.

It is as well for the aircraft industry and the airlines that most passengers do feel this way about air travel. In any case, those who want to enjoy flying for its own sake can still do so. All over the world, in tiny garages, workshops, and even bedrooms, enthusiasts are busy with carpenter's tools, glue-pots and paint-brushes, making tiny aeroplanes for fun. Often, these machines are powered by a converted motor-car engine, and cost no more than a small car to build and operate. In them, the amateur constructor-pilots can learn the true wonder of flying like the birds, free and exciting. In doing so, they see far more of the beauties of the earth beneath them than do passengers in 600 m.p.h. jet-liners, seven miles up and probably above the clouds.

The amateurs are seldom brilliant engineers, although the craftsmanship they put into their aeroplanes would do credit to any multi-million-pound company. Nor are they usually wealthy, and their aircraft work has to be a spare-time activity. Their aeroplanes are often extremely simple in construction, yet they fly beautifully.

Why then, did it take thousands of years and endless thought and effort by the world's great scientists and most imaginative engineers, with plenty of time and money at their disposal, before anyone could build an aeroplane capable of even twelve seconds of shaky flight?

The birds are to blame. They made flying look so easy that most would-be airmen tried to copy them, by building wings of wood, feathers and fabric and jumping off the nearest high place with the wings strapped to their arms. Flapping their wings desperately, the bird-men normally flew only one way—vertically downward. It was all very frustrating and humiliating, especially as such spectacles drew large crowds, who predicted the outcome far more accurately than did the 'bird-men'. They went home afterwards satisfied at having had a good afternoon's sport, and more convinced than ever that if God had meant men to fly He would have given them wings.

Bird-men who were lucky enough to walk away from the tangled wreckage of their wings often thought up original excuses for their failure. John Damian, after crashing to the ground beneath the walls of Stirling Castle, instead of flying to France as planned, said that he had made the mistake of using feathers from chickens, which are ground birds, instead of eagles' feathers.

Nor were birds the only inspiration of those who tried to flap their way to fame in the air. Historians and storytellers had glorified the exploits of men like Daedalus and his son, Icarus, who escaped imprisonment by King Minos of Crete by flying over the sea to Sicily. Icarus suffered a structural failure en route, when he became so exhilarated with the sensation of flying that he climbed too near the sun, which melted the wax holding his wings together, so that he crashed and was killed. Daedalus reached his destination and the generations of bird-men who tried to follow him clearly considered that flying's initial 50 per cent safety record was not too frightening.

Unfortunately, the record did not improve, and a steadily-mounting number of experimenters followed Icarus rather

The tradition of the early bird-men, who sought a purely personal kind of flying, is maintained by the amateur constructor-pilots of today. All over the world, in workshops, garages, even bedrooms, they are busy with saw, glue-pot and welding torch, building light aeroplanes of all shapes and sizes. Some, like *Puppy Feet*, the Meyer Little Toot single-seat biplane built by Walter Prell of Des Plaines, Illinois, U.S.A., *top right*, are beautiful to look at and to fly. Others, such as the flapping-wing machine shown in the lower illustration, prove that the centuries-old longing to fly like the birds lives on in a jet age. This particular aircraft, built at a cost of £5 by Mick Walton of Taunton, Somerset, did not leave the ground; but many people still believe that flying by human muscle-power is possible.

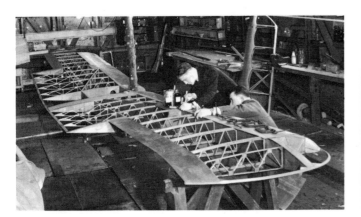

Kai Ka'us, King of Persia hundreds of years before Christ, was not a do-it-yourself bird-man. He took the easy way out, by harnessing four large birds to his flying throne. Ancient chronicles depict the monarch prior to take-off, with a bundle of arrows clasped in his hand, giving Kai Ka'us a firm claim to the title of world's first combat pilot. The less-happy looking bird-man in the upper right illustration is demonstrating that, although vertical take-off remained a dream, except in myth and legend, vertical landing was not only practicable but normal.

Even Britain had its Royal pioneer of flying, nearly 3,000 years ago. King Bladud, father of Shakespeare's King Lear, made wings with which he attempted to fly from the top of the temple of Apollo in what is now London. Describing Bladud's consequent demise, the 17th century poet John Taylor commented: 'On high the tempests have much power to wreck; then best to bide beneath and safest for the neck.' This implies that the king was the earliest known victim of air turbulence.

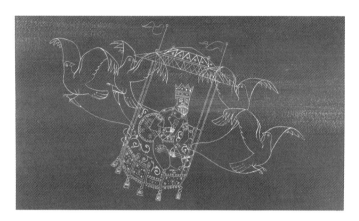

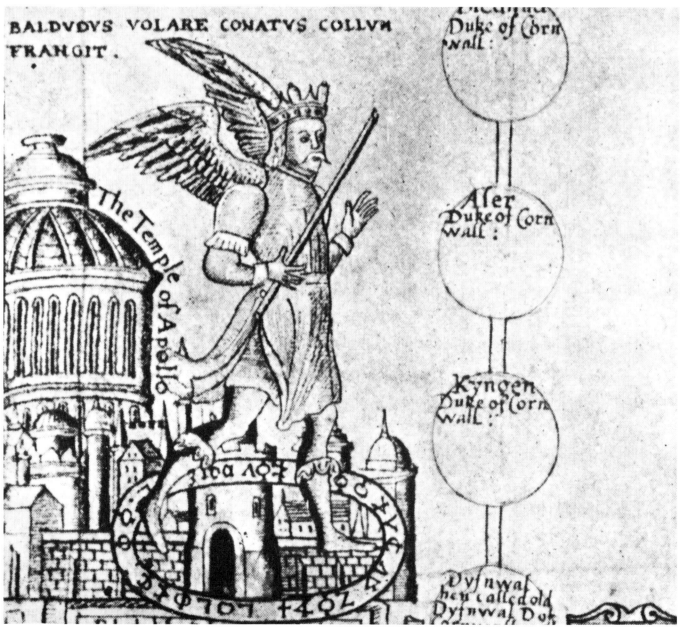

In the year 1505, Leonardo da Vinci directed all his talents as an artist and inventor to the task of solving the problems of human flight. Realising that man would never fly without mechanical aid, he wrote: 'A bird is an instrument working according to mathematical law, which instrument is within the capacity of man to reproduce in all its movements'. After a long study of the anatomy and movement of birds, he designed a flying machine with pulleys, cables and pivots that reproduced as nearly as possible the 'mechanism' of a bird. Although we know now that Leonardo's aircraft could never be made to work, he is remembered as the person who showed that flight would be achieved only when courage was allied to science.

than his father. Even the British royal family had to pay the price of pioneering.

According to ancient records or legends — the reader may take his pick—a young man named Bladud became the ninth king of Britain in the year 863 BC, at the time of the Old Testament prophet Elijah. He is said to have founded a university at Stamford in Lincolnshire and to have built the city of Bath, where he used his magical powers to create the hot springs. These powers do not seem to have done him much good when he joined the bird-men. Within seconds of launching himself on feathered wings from the temple of Apollo in Trinaventum (now London), he crashed into the temple, broke his neck, and was succeeded by his son, King Lear, of Shakespearean fame.

Oriental manuscripts are full of the most amazing stories of how their potentates travelled through the air in baskets and cages, lifted and towed by birds. Alexander the Great is reputed to have gone one better, by harnessing four of those fabulous winged creatures known as griffons to his flying machine. But even if anyone believed these stories, they probably considered it cheating to become airborne in this way. The birds and beasts that provided the motive power did the flying, not the passengers; so the bird-men kept trying, and dying.

Nearly 2,000 years after Bladud, in 1020 AD, an English monk named Oliver of Malmesbury jumped off a tower and survived, though not without injury. His exploit is recorded, with more imagination than factual accuracy, on the sign of a public house named *The Flying Monk*, not far from where he fell.

At about the same time, a man who is remembered only as 'the Saracen of Constantinople' killed himself in a similar experiment; yet, in some ways, he may have come nearer than any of his predecessors to discovering one of the keys to human flight. Instead of building flapping wings, he wore a voluminous cloak which was held open by stiffeners. In recent years, the American Clem Sohn and Leo Valentin of France both made many successful gliding flights with folding bat-wings not very different from the Saracen's cloak, although they too paid with their lives in the end.

Did any of the bird-men of ancient history succeed in matching even the modest achievements of Sohn and Valentin? Some authorities claim that they did. The Turks, in particular, believe that one of their countrymen, Hezarfen Celebi, launched himself from the high Tower of Galata on the banks of the Bosphorus in the early 17th century and landed safely in the market place at Scutari, several kilometres away. They even issued a postage stamp at the time of the Istanbul Civil Aviation Congress of 1950, showing him shortly after take-off. If Celebi's 'aircraft' really was

Today, the most up-to-date knowledge of aerodynamics and lightweight structures is being applied to the achievement of man-powered flight. Spurred on by the incentive of a £5,000 prize, offered for the first non-stop flight around two posts half-a-mile apart, several groups of enthusiasts in Britain have designed and built aeroplanes capable of being propelled into the air by one man. Typical of these machines was the Puffin, illustrated on the opposite page. Its wing span of 84 ft. was almost as great as that of a Trident three-jet airliner, yet the complete aircraft, without pilot, weighed a mere 118 lb. Built mainly of spruce and balsa wood, and covered with plastic film, it had a pedal-driven wheel and propeller. Its best flight covered 993 yd. in a straight line.

An earlier and less successful design was the Hartman ornithopter, *below*. It flew as a towed glider, as shown, but was too heavy to leave the ground with only a human power plant.

anything like that shown on the stamp, it might have had sufficient wing area to carry him the distance claimed, provided he kept the wings rigid and did not try to flap them; but we shall never know for certain whether this gallant Turk deserves more credit than he gets in the average aviation history book.

One inventor who is never forgotten was Leonardo da Vinci, painter of the *Mona Lisa*, scientist, architect, and designer of more mechanical masterpieces than almost any other single man in history. Overawed by his genius, some writers portray him as the inventor of the aeroplane, which he certainly was not. His designs for aircraft included one with fixed inner wings and flapping outer wings which might be made to work today, using our current know-how; but the rest relied on the same old man-powered flapping-wing ideas, and Leonardo's main contribution was the suggestion that muscle-power was insufficient by itself, even when using both arms and legs, and must be allied with mechanical devices before flight can be possible.

Even this suggestion was of no help to his contemporaries, or to anyone else for 450 years. The reason becomes apparent when we look at the time and money that are being poured into present-day attempts to fly even one mile in a man-powered aeroplane. The very latest lightweight materials and knowledge of mechanisms, structures and aerodynamics have not yet been sufficient for success, although this seems within reach. In Leonardo's time, there was not the slightest hope of getting off the ground and staying there.

With his unprecedented knowledge of anatomy, Leonardo might have been expected to realise this; but perhaps he was so full of wonder at what he learned about the human body that he could not see its weaknesses. Man's heart ticks over at 70 beats a minute; the sparrow's hits 800 beats a minute in flight. The bird's breathing system keeps pace with this, and a pigeon respires 400 times a minute in flight. To this 'high-revving' engine are allied large and heavy flying muscles, designed specially for the job and very different from a man's arm muscles. As for the bird's wings, by the time one has studied their complex mechanism and constantly changing form, the more clear it becomes that they could never be copied mechanically.

The dream of flying like the birds was, therefore, doomed to failure from the start. Just as land transport came to rely on the wheel, which has no counterpart in nature, so air travel had to find a substitute for the flapping wing. But before it did so, men learned to leave the ground by using an aircraft as impractical as one could imagine — a vehicle that could make only one-way journeys, where the wind chanced to carry it, as incapable of choosing its own course as a dandelion seed — yet, for all that, a craft that put man up among the birds for the first time.

HOT AIR AND HYDROGEN

From the start, there had been some would-be flyers who sought less-exhausting methods of getting airborne than by flapping their arms. As in the more recent case of space-flight, some of the earliest ideas came from science-fiction writers. For example, Cyrano de Bergerac, having noted how the morning dew rose when subjected to the sun's rays, suggested the building of an aircraft shaped like a huge glass ball containing dew. When exposed to the sun, he claimed, the dew would rise and the aircraft would take off vertically on journeys not merely on earth but to the other planets of the solar system.

He did not intend the suggestion to be taken seriously. Nevertheless, the idea of obtaining 'lift' in some such manner had been born, and people began considering if it might be possible for an aircraft to float in the air just as a heavy but hollow iron boat can be made to float on water. The problem was to find a way of making an aircraft lighter than the volume of air it displaced.

The break-through seemed to come with the invention of the air-pump by Otto von Guericke, in 1650. A Jesuit priest named Francesco de Lana-Terzi worked out that if he made a large copper globe of wafer-thin metal, and then used an air-pump to extract all the air from it, the globe would become considerably lighter than the air it displaced and would, therefore, float. In 1670, he produced the first-ever design for a lighter-than-air craft, consisting of a boat-shaped hull suspended from four of his copper globes, from which the air had been exhausted. With the lift problem solved, he added a mast and sail for propulsion and began to plan where he would go, by air, for his summer holidays.

Alas, there was a snag. It soon became clear that if he built the globes from sufficiently-thin metal to make the scheme possible, they would collapse when the air-pump got to work. On the other hand, if he built them strongly enough to avoid collapse, they would be too heavy. Far from appearing dismayed by this, he said that he was really very glad, adding:

'God would surely never allow such a machine to be successful, since it would cause much disturbance among the civil and political governments of mankind. Who can fail to see that no city would be proof against surprise, as the ship could at any time be brought above its squares, or even the courtyards of its dwellings, and come to earth so that its crew could land. In the case of ships that sail the sea, the aerial ship could be made to descend from the upper air to the level of their sails so that the rigging could be cut. Or even without descending so low, iron weights could be hurled down to wreck the ships and kill their crews; or the ships could be set on fire by fireballs and bombs. Not only ships, but houses, fortresses and cities could thus be destroyed, with the certainty that the airship would come to no harm, as the missiles could be thrown from a great height.'

De Lana may not have been much of an aircraft designer, but as a prophet of what military aviation would make possible three centuries later he was unsurpassed.

Monasteries were the centres of learning and scientific thought at this period, which explains why monks and priests dominate the story of flying from the 11th to the 18th centuries, except for the contributions of Leonardo da Vinci. After de Lana, the next important pioneer to emerge was another Jesuit Father named Laurenço de Gusmão. Most history books simply include a fanciful drawing of a machine named the *Passarola* (great bird), for which he was responsible, and imply that it was a ridiculous affair, incorporating every kind of 'lift producer' that Gusmão could think of, including feathered wings, a parachute, rarefied air, magnets and rockets. In fact, it was probably quite simple and straightforward, with a boat hull, birdlike tail, parachute-sail and two large flapping wings of wood and fabric. And there is good reason to believe that a model of the *Passarola*, possibly in the form of a fixed-wing glider, was flown successfully in Lisbon in 1709.

If this glider did fly, it was the first aeroplane in history. Nor did it mark the end of Gusmão's achievements, for it is almost certain that he demonstrated a model hot-air 'balloon' before the King of Portugal in that same year, preceding by 74 years the Montgolfier brothers, who are usually credited with inventing the balloon.

At least two reliable writers of the time have described

what happened. The aircraft appears to have consisted of a boat hull with a *Passarola*-type parachute-sail over the top. When a small fire was lit beneath it, the hot air rose, filled the sail and lifted the machine off the ground. It promptly flew into the curtains of the great hall where the experiment was being staged and set them on fire. In the words of the historians: 'It came to earth and caught fire when the materials became jumbled together. In descending and falling downwards, it set fire to some hangings and everything against which it knocked; but His Majesty was good enough not to take it ill.'

Kings and other rulers had to put up with a great deal in the years before anyone learned to fly. Every crackpot inventor invited the most important person available to witness demonstrations of his ideas, just in case one of them worked. So it is easy to imagine with what little enthusiasm the French King and Queen greeted the news that two of their subjects, named Joseph and Etienne Montgolfier, wished to prove that they had solved the problem of how to fly, in the garden of Versailles Palace on September 19, 1783. This time, however, they really were to be present at one of the great moments in aviation history.

The Montgolfiers had a paper-making business in the town of Annonay, near Lyons. It is unlikely that they had ever heard of Gusmão, and the inspiration for their balloon is said to have come to them while they were sitting by the

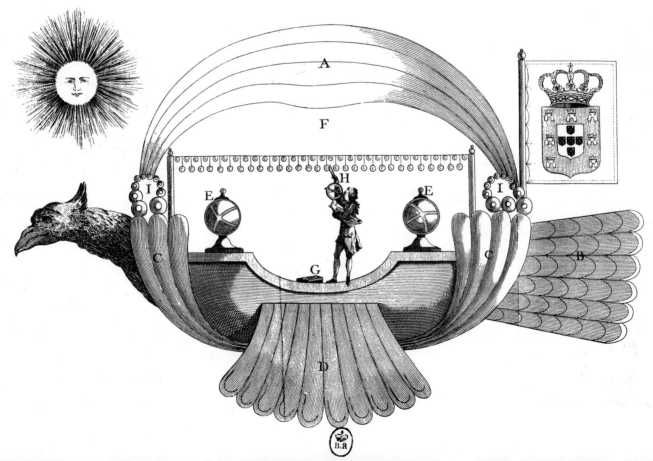

fire at home. Like countless other people, they were fascinated by the way in which little pieces of burned paper were wafted upward in the smoke, to disappear up the chimney. They did not know why this happened (because heated air becomes rarefied and rises, carrying the paper with it), but this was unimportant. They felt sure that if only they could trap enough of the 'gas' produced by a burning fire, they could use it to lift even men off the ground.

As a start, in mid-November 1782, they held a small silk bag over an indoor fire, open end downward. When they let go, it rose quickly to the ceiling. Tests with larger bags, of both silk and paper, followed. At last they felt ready to make their discovery public, and invited the leading citizens of Annonay to a demonstration flight on June 5, 1783. For the occasion, they made a huge spherical balloon, 38 feet in diameter, from linen panels, buttoned together and lined with paper to make it air-tight. When 'gas' from a fire of wool and straw had filled it out, they released it and the balloon soared upward to a height of more than 6,000 feet, before slowly descending as the hot air cooled, to land a mile and a half from its take-off point.

The good people of Annonay were dumb-founded at first, but soon realised the importance of what they had seen. The Montgolfiers became public heroes and an eye-

witness report of what had transpired was sent to the French Academy of Sciences. Instead of hurrying down to Annonay to see the miracle for themselves, the directors of the Academy gave their support to a public subscription, the funds from which were passed to the famous physicist J. A. C. Charles, with the request that he should get busy on producing a balloon. Although this may seem a little unfair to the Montgolfiers, it was to prove a far-sighted move; in any case, Etienne was invited to Paris to repeat his experiments before members of the Academy.

He built an enormous linen and paper balloon, 74 feet high, in a garden in the Rue de Montreuil, and demonstrated its lifting powers to representatives of the Academy, with the aircraft tethered to the ground so that it would not rise far enough to suffer damage or loss. Unfortunately, it began to pour with rain and Etienne soon found himself with only a soggy heap of linen and paper, a mere seven days before his appointment with the King and Queen at Versailles. Yet, he not only had a completely new balloon ready in time but, with Joseph's help, devised a method of suspending a wicker basket beneath it. Thus, when the big day came, Their Majesties were able to witness the first-ever aerial journey by living creatures. Whether the sheep, cock and duck housed in the basket appreciated the honour will never be known; at least they made a safe landing at the end of their eight-minute adventure.

Clearly, the next stage was to send up a man. But whom?

The Montgolfiers appear to have been perfectly satisfied with the fame that was now theirs as the creators of the first aerial vehicle, and had no obvious ambition to become the first aeronauts, although they did make one or two flights in later years. The King suggested that a condemned criminal might like to earn his freedom by volunteering. His advisers argued against this, saying that the Frenchman who went down in history as the first person to fly ought to be somebody worthy of the honour. And so, finally, the offer of a 29-year-old physician named Jean-François Pilâtre de Rozier to act as test pilot was accepted.

For such an auspicious event, the Montgolfiers produced a truly magnificent balloon. They used the 'gas-bag' of its predecessor but changed the shape, so that it was semi-spherical, with a pointed crown. A wicker gallery for one or two men was built around the open neck, inside which a brazier was slung so that the crew could renew the supply of hot air by stoking up in flight. The whole thing was finished in a striking blue and gold colour scheme, complete with the royal cipher, eagles, signs of the zodiac and smiling suns.

On October 15, 1783, in the presence of a vast crowd, de Rozier took his place in the basket of the balloon. A fire was lit under the open neck, and when the balloon had become inflated it was allowed to rise to a height of nearly 85 feet at the end of its tethering ropes. By stoking

the brazier with wool and straw, de Rozier managed to keep it up for 4 min 24 sec before descending to the wild applause of the Parisians.

In the (even then) inevitable press interview afterwards, it is recorded that: 'The intrepid adventurer, returning from the sky, assured his friends and the multitude, which had gazed on him with admiration, with wonder, and with fear, that he had not experienced the least inconvenience, either in going up, in remaining there, or in descending; no giddiness, no incommoding motion, no shock whatever.' Within a short time, de Rozier made five more flights, each a little higher than the last, climbing finally to 330 feet, complete with a passenger, but still tethered to the ground.

The next step was clearly a free flight, and on November 21, 1783, this was accomplished by de Rozier, with the Marquis d'Arlandes as passenger — in theory. In fact, it seems that the Marquis had to work his passage by keeping the fire stoked. He discovered this soon after take-off from the garden of the Royal Château de la Muette, in the Bois de Boulogne, when, in his own words: 'M. Pilâtre said, "You do nothing and we shall not mount." "Pardon me," I replied, "but it is necessary to reassure those unhappy human beings whom we have left below, in less enjoyable circumstances than ours." I then threw a truss of straw upon the fire.' A little later, when sparks from the brazier began to make the balloon smoulder, he had to deal with the emergency with a wet sponge. It was, therefore, quite an adventurous journey, which lasted 25 minutes and took the two aeronauts right across Paris and deposited them $5\frac{1}{2}$ miles from their starting point.

After centuries of sacrifice and endeavour, man had finally become airborne. *Montgolfières* (as hot-air balloons were known) were, admittedly, frail and somewhat hazardous devices, lacking any form of propulsion or steering, so that they could travel only where the wind carried them. It was not quite flying in the manner that most men had longed to fly, like the birds, but it was a start.

Furthermore, an improved vehicle was already on the way, thanks to the publicly-financed research of Prof. J.A.C. Charles. From the start, he had sought a more efficient lifting medium than the 'Montgolfier gas' used in hot-air balloons, which had to be renewed so dangerously in flight. Seventeen years earlier, the English chemist Henry Cavendish had discovered a gas which he called 'inflammable air' and which we now know as hydrogen. Weight of 1,000 cu. ft. of this gas was a mere 5.3 lb., compared with 76 lb. for an equivalent volume of air. It was clear, therefore, to Prof. Charles that 'inflammable air' would be ideal as a substitute for 'Montgolfier gas'. What is more, it could be sealed inside the balloon instead of needing constant replenishment in an open-ended gas-bag.

To test his theories, Charles enlisted the help of two

During the 1914-18 War, captive balloons were used by both sides as aerial platforms from which the movements of enemy ground forces could be observed. The sausage shape and lobes of the balloons helped to keep them steady at the end of their tethering cables, but they provided sitting targets for the pilots of fighter aeroplanes once machine-guns firing incendiary bullets had become standard armament for combat aircraft.

brothers named Robert, who had perfected a method of rubberising silk to make it leak-proof. Together, they designed and built a spherical balloon, 13 ft. in diameter, with a stop-cock for inflation at the bottom. At 5 p.m. on August 27, 1783, some three weeks before the Montgolfiers' 'Royal Command performance' at Versailles, a cannon was fired and the balloon, without a pilot, was released from the Champ de Mars, near Paris.

Fearing that the citizens of neighbouring villages might be alarmed if they saw unidentified flying objects of this kind bearing down on their homes, the government had issued a proclamation stating that: 'Anyone who shall see in the sky such a globe, which resembles the moon in eclipse, should be aware that, far from being an alarming phenomenon, it is only a machine that cannot possibly cause any harm, and which will someday prove useful to the needs of society.'

Alas, the balloon reached the village of Gonesse before the proclamation. Terrified by the shape which descended on them from the stormy sky, the inhabitants kept a respectful distance until one brave soul ventured near enough to shoot it. Then, as it wheezed and wilted before their eyes, they rushed in with flails and pitchforks, only to be driven back by the stench of the dying monster. Not until the remains had been tied to a horse's tail and torn to shreds as the beast galloped across the fields, did they feel safe.

For Charles, the 15-mile flight represented a considerable success and, backed by a further public subscription, he began work on a full-size, man-carrying *Charlière* (hydrogen balloon). This remarkable aircraft was so ingeniously designed that even today sporting balloons do not differ from it in their essential details. It consisted of a rubberised-silk gas-bag, or envelope, $27\frac{1}{2}$ feet in diameter, with a filling-tube and gas-vent, to let out gas for descent, at the bottom. The top half was covered with a net, supporting a hoop around the equator, from which a wicker-work basket was suspended on ropes.

In this balloon, Charles and Marie-Noel Robert made a highly-successful two-hour flight on December 1, 1783, and this marked the true beginning of ballooning as a sport. After landing, Charles decided to go up again by himself. Relieved of the weight of the second man, the balloon shot up to a height of more than 9,000 feet. Despite the intense cold and sharp earache caused by this rapid ascent, Charles did not omit to take readings with scientific instruments on board, while valving off gas as quickly as seemed prudent. Some writers say that he was so frightened by the experience, with some justification, that he never went up again. Whether or not this is true, it is indisputable that his is the greatest name in the early history of lighter-than-air flight.

Ballooning quickly became a sport and a spectacle all over the world. Professional aeronauts, both men and

By the beginning of the 20th century, ballooning had become a fashionable and respectable sport. Even airships, fitted with engines and able to be steered in flight, were considered acceptable; but society shunned the noisy, dirty and rather dangerous aeroplanes which certain misguided men were trying to persuade to leave the ground.

The upper illustration on this page shows the airship in which Ernest Willows of Cardiff flew 140 miles from his home town to the Crystal Palace, London, in 10 hours on August 6-7, 1910.

In the following month, he flew it from the Crystal Palace to St. Paul's Cathedral and back, before enlarging it and using it for the first cross-Channel flight by a British airship. In its original form, this Willows Airship No. 2 was 86 ft. long and was powered by a 35 h.p. J.A.P. engine.

The lower illustration depicts a balloon ascent during a King's College fete at the Crystal Palace.

The free balloon shown left was used only to add a little more humour to the 20th Century-Fox film, *Those Magnificent Men in their Flying Machines*. Ballooning is, however, regaining some of its old popularity as a sport.

First heavier-than-air aeroplane to fly was the model glider, *right*, built in 1804 by Sir George Cayley. Although little more than a kite mounted on a stick, with a movable tail, it established the configuration of a modern aeroplane and was itself scaled up into a glider large enough to carry a boy.

1836. Even this seems a mere hop by comparison with John Wise's 804-mile journey from St. Louis to Henderson, New York, in 1859. These were exciting, inspiring achievements, but the balloon remained a thoroughly impractical vehicle, as the only way of getting it back home was to deflate it and pack it for transport by road, rail or ship.

Inevitably, however, it was not long before somebody found a military use for ballooning. As early as June 26, 1794, Captain Coutelle of the French army made ascents totalling several hours in a captive (i.e. tethered) balloon during the Battle of Fleurus in Belgium. The information on enemy troop movements that he signalled down to General Jourdan's Moselle army contributed greatly to the French victory.

In almost every war that followed, balloons played a part. Their main disadvantages were that, for many years, they had to be accompanied by a heavy gas generator, acid cart and other gear, took about three hours to inflate and were almost uncontrollable in a high wind. Controllability improved in 1897, when a German officer named von Perseval invented the sausage-shape *Drachen* balloon, with tail-fins to keep it pointing into wind. Later, the use of compressed gas in cylinders removed many of the transport and inflation problems, and balloons were used for observation on a large scale by both sides in the 1914-18 War. But by World War II they had become so vulnerable that they could be used only in unpiloted form as anti-aircraft barrage balloons.

Attempts were made to improve their usefulness by making them controllable and increasing their speed. A great English pioneer named Sir George Cayley, of whom we shall hear more later, suggested the use of a streamlined gas-bag and even introduced steam-driven propellers for propulsion and steering on his airship project of 1837. But it was not until 1850 that such a craft was built, in model form, by Pierre Jullien of France. His little clockwork-powered *Précurseur* inspired the full-size steam-powered airship in which Henri Giffard flew from Paris to Trappes at the breakneck speed of 6 m.p.h. in 1852. This was real progress, even if the craft was only partially controllable.

The first completely successful airship, able to be steered on any course, irrespective of wind, was the electrically-powered *La France*, built by Renard and Krebs in 1884. All that was needed then was a more efficient power plant, and this came when the little Brazilian pioneer, Alberto Santos-Dumont, fitted a petrol-engine to an airship in 1898 and, later, flew an improved version round the Eiffel Tower in Paris.

But, by then, the petrol-engine was about to make possible a different kind of aircraft, and the kind of flying which men had tried vainly to achieve since the time of Bladud.

women, thrilled crowds by making public ascents. When this began to lose its appeal, they added to the excitement by such stunts as ascending on horse-back, making parachute-jumps and letting off fireworks from the balloon in flight, at night.

First to attempt a really ambitious international journey were Jean-Pierre Blanchard of France and Dr John Jeffries, an American, who set out to cross the Channel, from Dover, on January 7, 1785. They reached France, but only after dumping overboard everything on which they could lay their hands, including life-jackets, a bottle of brandy, anchors, oars, food, their coats, and even Blanchard's trousers, to lighten the balloon when it began to lose height over the sea.

Pilâtre de Rozier tried to make a crossing in the opposite direction, with a companion, on June 15 of the same year. For the attempt, he built a strange craft consisting of a spherical hydrogen balloon on top of a cylindrical hot-air balloon. He must have been aware of the danger of having an open fire near so inflammable a gas as hydrogen, but he ignored it, and both men died when the balloon collapsed near the French coast. So the first man to fly became also the first man to die in an air accident.

When cities began to adopt coal gas for lighting, this gradually replaced hydrogen in sporting balloons. First to use the new gas was Charles Green, who made a superb flight of 480 miles to Weilburg in Germany in November

FLEDGELINGS

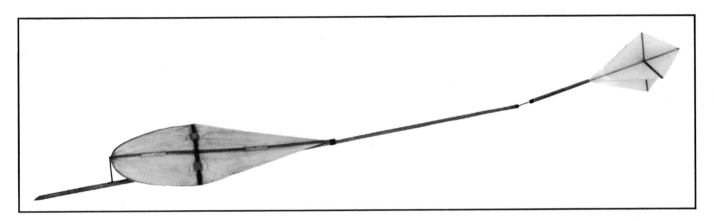

Among the crowd that witnessed the release of Professor Charles' first unmanned hydrogen balloon from the Champ de Mars, in August 1783, was the great American scientist and diplomat, Benjamin Franklin. Someone nearby asked, with a touch of sarcasm: 'What possible use is a balloon?' Franklin replied: 'Of what use is a new-born baby?'

As we have seen, this particular baby never grew into a really useful member of the community; neither did it develop along aggressive lines, as de Lana had feared. Although he was never to know, Franklin had held in his own hands, many times, the key to a completely different type of aircraft that was destined to be both useful and aggressive.

The experiment for which he is best remembered is that in which he proved the relationship between lightning and electricity, by flying a kite in a thunderstorm. It is unlikely that he thought much about why the kite flew. After all, the Chinese had been flying kites since time immemorial and they were an accepted part of life — toys in the West, even if they were taken more seriously in the Far East.

The person who really began to study kites closely was Sir George Cayley, the Yorkshire baronet whose ideas on airship design have already been mentioned. In 1799, at the age of 26, he designed an aircraft which was very different from anything that anyone had proposed before. For the first time, lift and thrust were separated. Instead

of flapping wings, his aeroplane had a fixed wing of wood and canvas, beneath which the pilot sat in a boat-shape fuselage. To control the direction of flight, he moved a cruciform tail by means of a tiller. To propel the aircraft, there were two large paddles operated by an oar-type mechanism.

Cayley knew that a cambered wing gave more lift than a flat one, but usually achieved this on his aircraft by fitting sail-type wings that were curved by airflow filling them out, rather than rigid cambered wings. His studies also taught him the value of streamlining, and that the simplest way of achieving lateral stability was by having the wings set at a dihedral angle (i.e. forming an almost flat V in head-on view).

To test his theories, he turned to the kite — the 'wing' that had existed for centuries without its significance being recognised. He fastened it to a five-foot-long pole with the front of the kite propped up, so that there was an angle of 6° between kite and pole (the angle of incidence). The cruciform tail was attached to the pole by a universal joint, so that it could be moved from side to side and up and down, to control the direction of flight. In other words, he produced the basic wing/fuselage/tail unit layout of a modern aeroplane — and it worked.

Cayley knew that the three essentials for a heavier-than-air machine were stability, so that the aircraft would stay

straight and level in normal flight, an efficient control system, and some form of power plant. The movable tail on his glider provided control; he knew how to increase stability by the use of dihedral, although this was not necessary on so simple a device as his kite-glider; and he used gravity instead of a mechanical power plant in these first simple experiments with his model glider.

'It was very pretty to see it sail down a steep hill,' he wrote later, 'And it gave the idea that a larger instrument would be a better and safer conveyance down the Alps than even the surefooted mule... The least inclination of the tail towards the right or left made it shape its course like a ship by the rudder.'

Within five years, Cayley had scaled up this model into a full-size glider with a wing area of 300 square feet — more than twice as much as on many modern lightplanes. On more than one occasion, he allowed small boys to glide downhill for a few yards on this aircraft; but he realised from the start that any major success in heavier-than-air flight would have to await the invention of a powerful, lightweight power plant.

For many years, he turned his attention primarily to airship design; but his theories were not forgotten and they inspired a man named William Samuel Henson to produce in 1843 one of the most significant aeroplane designs in history. He called it the Aerial Steam Carriage and, although primitive in detail, it was of far better design than many of the aeroplanes that were to succeed in staggering into the air sixty years later. In fact, its basic layout, with fuselage slung under a monoplane wing (of 150 ft span!), a movable tail unit, nose-wheel undercarriage and two pusher propellers, was similar to that of a conventional aeroplane of the present day.

What is more, anyone able to visit Britain's National Aeronautical Collection in the Science Museum, London, can still see the actual 20-ft-span scale model of the Aerial Steam Carriage that Henson built, with the help of his friend John Stringfellow. That such a historical model, of the first-ever design for a complete powered aeroplane, should still exist nearly 130 years later is remarkable. Even more astonishing is the genius of its designer. The wing, in particular, is a double-surface, cambered structure, with sturdy spars and deep ribs, just like that of a modern aeroplane.

Why is it, then, that Henson did not build a full-size version and become the first man to fly in a powered heavier-than-air machine? One reason is that the model did not work. When tested in 1847, it ran down an inclined launching ramp to gather speed and shot off the end, into the air. But the steam engine that drove its two propellers was too heavy and gave too little power. The model succeeded only in making a short hop, losing height all the time.

Even worse, Henson had let his enthusiasm run riot by trying to form a company to build and operate Aerial

Steam Carriages on passenger services. He issued to the press fantastic drawings showing the machine in flight over London, Paris and even the Pyramids. The reaction was inevitable. In the newspapers and even in Parliament, Henson and his Aerial Transit Company were subjected to such ridicule that, when the model failed to fly, he emigrated to America and made no further contributions to the history of flying.

The basic reason for Henson's failure was that the Aerial Steam Carriage was half a century before its time. With a few minor changes based on Cayley's research, such as giving the wings dihedral to improve stability, the model might well have been made aerodynamically sound enough to fly; but it would still have lacked a suitable engine. Throughout the remainder of the 19th century, every aircraft designer, no matter how brilliant his ideas, was to encounter this same lack of a lightweight, efficient power plant; and it is safe to guess that the first powered aeroplane flight might have taken place twenty, thirty, even fifty years earlier had the petrol-engine been invented at that time.

Steam-engines were no substitute, however skilfully they were constructed. Henson's colleague, Stringfellow, discovered this when he continued experimenting, first with a 10-ft. monoplane very like the Aerial Steam Carriage, in 1848, and then with a triplane model twenty years later.

Next great pioneer after Cayley was William Samuel Henson.
With John Stringfellow, he designed a remarkable Aerial Steam
Carriage, *lower picture*, the general layout of which was similar
to that of the conventional aeroplane of today. A 20 ft. model,
built by the two men, failed to fly. Discouraged by this,
and by public ridicule, Henson gave up his experiments.
Stringfellow carried on alone and built several more models,
including that shown in the upper illustration. Launched
from a wire, it achieved no more than a steadily descending flight.

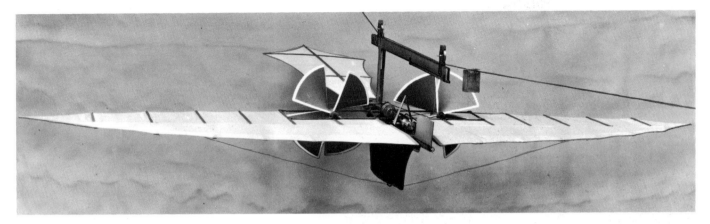

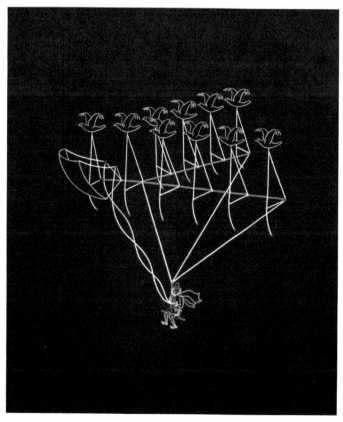

Even after Borelli had explained, in 1680, that man lacked sufficient strenght ever to sustain his weight in the air unaided, there were still bird-men willing to try. As late as 1742, the 62-year-old Marquis de Bacqueville, *left*, attempted to flap his way over the River Seine in Paris and was lucky to escape with only a broken leg.

Science-fiction writers continued to put their faith in more glamorous methods of flying. Francis Godwin, Bishop of Hereford, told how his hero, Domingo Gonsales, trained geese to lift him into the air, *below left*.

The fact that so many of the gods of primitive peoples, all over the world, were imagined as winged beings shows how strong man's longing to fly has always been. Unable to fly himself, he regarded the ability to fly as proof of supernatural powers.

First definite design for a lighter-than-air craft, foreshadowing the balloon and airship, was de Lana's project of 1679, *below*. By extracting the air from four large copper globes, he believed he could make them lighter than air so that they would float on the atmosphere as a ship floats on water.

Sir George Cayley's work reached a triumphant climax in 1853 when, as an old man of 80, he was able to send his reluctant coachman gliding across a small valley on his Yorkshire estate. Four years earlier, he had built the triplane shown below and had allowed a boy to skim down a hillside in it. So, by the mid-1850s, anyone taking advantage of the theories and discoveries of Cayley might have succeeded in building a flyable aircraft. All that was needed was a powerful, lightweight engine to make possible the progress from gliding to powered flight. Lack of this engine was destined to delay such progress for half a century.

First powered aeroplane to leave the ground with a pilot on board was the du Temple monoplane, shown in the upper of the two illustrations below. It became airborne only after gathering impetus down an inclined ramp. A similar ramp enabled the big monoplane built by Alexander Mozhaisky to make a brief powered hop in Russia in 1884, *lower picture.*

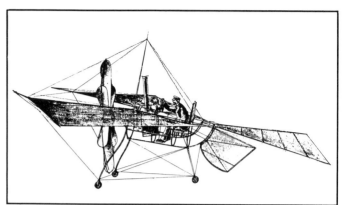

Launched from a wire, they made a pretence at flying; but neither advanced the progress of aviation significantly.

By the time Henson and Stringfellow were building and testing their models in the 1840s, Cayley was getting an old man, but not too old to forget the thrill of seeing his glider sailing down the hillside on his Yorkshire estate. So, in 1849, at the age of 76, he built a glider which, in some respects, was strangely reminiscent of Gusmão's *Passarola*. The boat-shape hull, bird-tail and flapping-wings were still there, as was the wing, supported rather like the canopy of a four-poster bed. The big difference was that Cayley's careful research and inherent genius as an engineer enabled him to produce a full-size version that was entirely practical.

We know what that aircraft of 1849 looked like, as he left quite good sketches of it—so good that the Australian airline Qantas was able to have a model of it made for inclusion in its unique collection of replicas of aircraft that marked real milestones in flying history.

As can be seen in the illustration of the Qantas model, it had triplane 'sail-wings' and was intended to be controlled by the tail unit. The flappers were expected, rather optimistically, to offset the absence of an engine by providing at least a token propulsive power. Weight of the whole thing was a mere 132½ lb; so, with 338 sq. ft. of wing area, there is little doubt that this strange-looking machine would have been able to lift a man; but once again it seems that

the only passenger it ever carried was a boy. We don't known why, but it may not be hard to guess...

One can imagine this rather distinguished old gentleman telling one of his young relations or friends about the time, many years ago, when youngsters used to fly a few yards down the hill in his early glider, and then showing the boy the much finer aircraft that he had just built. 'Please, Sir George, please let me have a ride...' At last, Cayley might have given in and let the boy fly briefly down the hillside, with some of his servants puffing along beside the glider, holding the structure or restraining it with ropes to ensure it would not go too fast or too far.

The one person who made a real flight in a Cayley glider—perhaps even crossed a small valley in it—was much less excited and eager than the boy in our little story; but he was a conscripted pilot rather than a volunteer, which always makes a difference.

The date was 1853, in Sir George's 80th year. Profiting from experience with the boy-carrier, which he called 'the old flyer', he had designed and built a 'new flyer'. With the impatience often felt by the elderly, he is said to have ordered his coachman, himself no young man, to act as test pilot on a demonstration flight. It is easy to imagine how reluctantly this man clambered into the boat-shape carriage, by no means reassured by Cayley's words that, as the controls were locked, he would not have to worry about keeping

Some people still claim that Clement Ader of France was the first man to make proper powered flights, in the two bat-winged, steam-powered aircraft shown below. Certainly, he made brief hops in the *Eole* (*top picture*) in 1890 and this must be acknowledged as the first aircraft able to raise itself from the ground entirely under its own power. But the requirements for true flight are that it should be both sustained and controlled. Ader covered, at best, about 150 feet in his hops and neither the *Eole* nor the later *Avion III* (*lower picture*) embodied a practical control system.

straight and level but need only work the bell-crank levers to flap the wings.

The 'new flyer' must have made quite a picture as, after a push, it left the hillside and glided across the little valley, to make a roughish landing on the other side. Red-faced from his exertion, the coachman is reported to have said: 'Please, Sir George, I wish to give notice. I was hired to drive and not to fly.' Little did he realise that his exploit would go down as the first man-carrying aeroplane flight in history.

Biggest tragedy of the Cayley story is that nearly a century was to pass before his work received full recognition. Today, he is acknowledged throughout the world as 'the father of aeronautics', the inventor of the aeroplane and founder of the science of aerodynamics. Had this been acknowledged sooner, many worthless aeroplanes would not have been built and many lives would not have been lost in trying to make them fly.

Of all the people who tried to succeed, where Henson and Stringfellow had failed, in the last half of the 19th century, fewer than a dozen helped to pave the way for the ultimate success of the American Wright brothers. Even the achievements of these few pioneers were often of more psychological than practical value.

First on the list was a French naval officer named Félix du Temple de La Croix. On May 2, 1857, this man patented the design for a steam-powered monoplane, with wing

dihedral for stability, tail control surfaces, a tricycle undercarriage and the engine and propeller in the best possible place—at the front. He even suggested that it should be made of aluminium, like modern aeroplanes, although this was then a very new material.

A model of this aircraft, powered first by a clockwork motor and later by a small steam-engine, was the first in the world to take off under its own power, fly without losing height and then land properly. Nor was this all. Some 17 years later, in 1874, du Temple built a full-size version of his design, powered by a hot-air engine, and persuaded a young sailor to have a shot at flying this, at Brest. It probably ran down a slope to gather speed before making a short hop through the air, which is very different from a properly controlled and sustained flight. Nevertheless, it was a start—the first time a man-carrying powered aircraft had left the ground.

Nobody has tried to claim that du Temple ought to replace the Wright brothers as the first person to build a practical aeroplane; but there have been plenty of other candidates for the honour. For many years, the Russians claimed that an aeroplane designed by one of their countrymen, Alexander Mozhaisky, made a genuine flight in 1884, piloted by a man named Golubev. They produced picture postcards showing the big machine soaring above the heads of a crowd of Russian citizens, with a portrait

The illustrations on this and the opposite page sum up the progress towards powered flight that had been made by the mid 18th Century. The first essential, of finding a lifting force capable of raising an aircraft into the air had been solved — rather unsatisfactorily — by the invention of the Montgolfier hot-air balloon, *lower picture on this page*. A more practical solution had existed in a primitive form for centuries, in the shape of the kite, *top picture*, *opposite page*. After taking a kite as the basis for his earliest glider, Sir George Cayley evolved more efficient wing shapes and was able eventually to build his successful boy-carrying, *lower picture*, *opposite page*, and man-carrying gliders in 1849-53. Unfortunately, the most efficient power plant available throughout most of the 19th century was the too-heavy steam engine, shown diagramatically in the cutaway drawing of Henson's Aerial Steam Carriage, *upper picture on this page*. Aeroplane designers were, therefore, still confronted with the major problems of finding a suitable lightweight power plant and devising a workable control system for when they did succeed in becoming airborne.

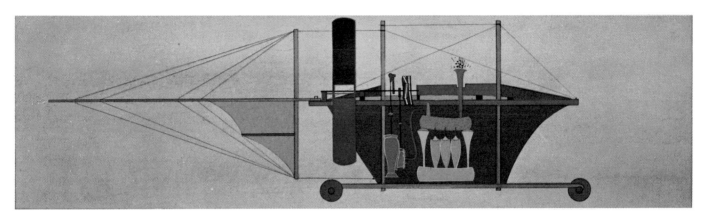

of the bearded Mozhaisky in one corner, looking very pleased with himself.

In fact, he had good reason to do so. His aeroplane, with its large wings, tail control surfaces and three propellers, driven by two British-built steam-engines of 20 h.p. and 10 h.p. respectively, was quite a workmanlike design. And there seems little doubt that it made a brief hop after taking off down a wooden ramp. As it weighed nearly a ton, Mozhaisky could scarcely have hoped for more on the power of two small steam engines.

By comparison, the two strange bat-wing aeroplanes built by Clement Ader of France look far less convincing; yet they achieved even more. On October 9, 1890, Ader started up the 20 h.p. steam-engine of the first of them, the *Eole*, and hopped off the ground without the assistance of a ramp. He claimed later to have flown more than 150 feet, but one has only to look at the *Eole* to see that it could never make a proper controlled flight. The second machine, *Avion III*, was even less successful. Nonetheless, Ader deserves his place in history as the first man to build a man-carrying aircraft able to lift itself from the ground under its own steam, however briefly.

Sir Hiram Maxim achieved similar success in 1894 with a fantastic structure of steel tube and canvas powered by two 180-h.p. steam-engines. Nobody can accuse Sir Hiram of not thinking big. His aeroplane weighed 3½ tons, spanned 104 ft. and was as tall as a house. Being a cautious type, he arranged for it to run along a track and had wooden guard rails above the wheels to ensure that it could not lift itself more than a few inches. On the day of its big test, it developed so much lift that it broke free of one of the guard rails and half flew before crashing to a stop. Whether Sir Hiram found the experience unnerving we are not told, but he certainly did not attempt to fly the machine again.

He was a great engineer, with many fine inventions to his credit; but his aeroplane was a scientific absurdity. The people who made *real* progress in the second half of the 19th century were those who accepted the fact that the steam-engine was useless and decided to concentrate on the aerodynamics of flight, to get the aeroplane right, in the hope that by the time they did so somebody would devise a suitable engine for it.

The seeds of this scientific approach were planted on January 12, 1866, when six men gathered at the residence of His Grace the Duke of Argyll to establish the Aeronautical Society of Great Britain (now the Royal Aeronautical Society). Their aim was to try and persuade people to accept aeronautics as a serious science in an age when, in its only practical form of ballooning, it had degenerated into a circus stunt.

They performed their task well. At the Society's very first meeting, Francis Wenham read a paper on 'Aerial Locomotion' which confirmed Cayley's theories and laid down almost every basic principle on which the theory and practice of heavier-than-air flight are founded. He built a wind-tunnel for the Society and showed how it could be used to improve wing design.

To the theories of Cayley and Wenham were added in 1890 the practical genius of a German named Otto Lilienthal. Realising the inadequacy of existing engines, he concentrated on building and flying gliders. In doing so, he became the first man to fly consistently well and with confidence. In six years, he made literally thousands of flights in his beautiful bird-like craft of peeled willow wands covered with waxed linen cloth. Carefully tabulating the results of his tests, he gradually improved the design until he could make flights of 300 to more than 750 ft. at heights up to 75 ft. Unfortunately, he made the fatal mistake of relying on movements of his body in the air to control the aircraft's flight; and on August 9, 1896, he lost control, crashed, and died on the following day. His last words were: 'Sacrifices must be made.'

Over in America, two brothers named Wilbur and Orville Wright, who had a cycle business in Dayton, Ohio, did not agree. They believed that an aeroplane could be built and flown without any great risk, provided the job was tackled scientifically. And, as so often happens if one believes in something strongly enough, they went on and did it.

Sir Hiram Maxim, famous as the inventor of the modern machine-gun, tried to offset the weight of the steam-engine by building an aeroplane with huge lifting surfaces. Completed in 1894, his biplane, *opposite page and top left picture below*, spanned 104 ft. and weighed 3½ tons. By skilful design, each of the 180-h.p. steam-engines was made light enough to be supported by Maxim, *top right picture*, and this enabled him to come nearer to success than any of his predecessors, with the possible exception of Ader.

To prevent the huge aircraft from leaving the ground inadvertently during its initial trials, it was designed to run along a steel railway track fitted with wooden guard rails to hold down the wheels. However, the wings developed so much lift that, even with four persons on board, the biplane broke free of the guard rails when it reached a speed of 40 m.p.h., after a 200-yd. run.

Recognising the inadequacy of existing engines, Otto Lilienthal concentrated on building gliders, *lower picture*. He made more than two thousand successful flights before crashing fatally in 1896.

THE FIRST 'MAGNIFICENT MEN'

Wilbur and Orville Wright knew all about Lilienthal. A fellow-American named Octave Chanute had been so inspired by the achievements of the German pioneer that he tried to carry on where Lilienthal ended. More important, he wrote a book called *Progress in Flying Machines* in which he listed all worthwhile achievements and ideas in aeronautical design up to that time. The Wrights studied the book meticulously, wrote to Chanute for more information, and decided to build and fly a powered aeroplane.

From the start, they had no doubt that they would be successful. Lilienthal had proved conclusively that flying was possible. Having learned all they could about his successes and failures, and those of the other early experimenters, they realised that the main problem was still to achieve stability and control in flight. Finding a suitable engine could come later. Anyway, it was less of a problem now that the petrol-engine had been perfected.

No reckless do-or-die characters, they were quite prepared to spend several years at the job. After all, people had been trying to fly for centuries without success; it was hardly likely that anybody would beat them now. This was very nearly the only mistake they made.

In Britain, a young ex-sailor named Percy Pilcher had also been bitten by the flying bug and had travelled over to Germany to watch Lilienthal gliding gracefully from the top of the artificial hill he had made near Berlin, specially for his experiments. The German must have been impressed by his visitor, as he allowed Pilcher to try out some of his gliders.

On returning home, Pilcher began building gliders very like those of Lilienthal, but with one important difference. By fitting them with wheels, he made them much easier to move around on the ground. Most famous of his gliders was the Hawk, first flown in 1896. In it he made many fine flights of up to 250 yards, after perfecting the technique of getting his assistants to tow him into the air at the end of a line — a method still used today, although with a rather better kind of cable than the fishing line used by Pilcher!

Before long, he decided to fit a small engine to one of his gliders, to see if he could produce a practical powered aeroplane. There was nothing suitable on the market, so he had to build his own and by 1899 had completed a neat little oil engine of 4-h.p., designed to drive a 48-in. propeller. Alas, it was never even fitted to an aircraft. If it had been, Britain might have become the birthplace of powered flight, even though the aircraft concerned might still have relied for control on the unsatisfactory technique of moving the pilot's body from side to side and fore and aft as he hung beneath it.

On September 30, 1899, Pilcher took two of his gliders to Lord Braye's home, near Market Harborough. As they had been soaked by rain, he decided to fly only his trusty old Hawk. At the first attempt, the line snapped as a team of horses towed him off the ground. Undeterred, Pilcher tried again, but a bamboo strut in the tail unit broke in the air, the Hawk crashed, and two days later Britain's only real challenger to the Wrights died of his injuries.

Clearly, it could be only a matter of time before somebody finished the job started by Cayley, Henson, du Temple, Lilienthal and Pilcher. Back at the turn of the century, it may have been difficult to see all the pieces of the jigsaw falling into place. With the advantage of carefully-sifted and recorded history at our finger-tips, we can see now that anyone who had combined the aerodynamic theories of Cayley and Wenham with the experience of real flying gained by Lilienthal, the type of aero-engine built by Pilcher, and the box-kite wing structure invented in far-off Australia by Lawrence Hargrave might have ended up with a practical aeroplane.

Perhaps the biggest danger was that somebody would succeed in being first in an aeroplane that was not really practical. For example, if Maxim or Ader had flown convincingly, it might have set other pioneers chasing along a false trail that would have put back real flying for ten or twenty years. One such person was a German civil servant named Karl Jatho, who built a machine in 1903 that was little more than a powered kite with a 9-h.p. petrol engine. A glance at pictures of his machine is sufficient to show that it could hardly have been controllable and could never have been developed into an aeroplane capable of flying

Lilienthal's work was carried on by men like Percy Pilcher in England and Octave Chanute in America. These pictures of a Chanute glider exhibited at the World's Fair at St. Louis in 1903 show the progress that had been made by then in developing an efficient rigid wing structure, with cambered surfaces of the kind suggested originally by Cayley. The tail surfaces were rubber-sprung to damp out gusts in flight, but Chanute continued to rely on movements of the pilot's body for primary control and stability.

An invention which was to have a great influence on early aircraft design came from far-off Australia, where Lawrence Hargrave perfected the box-kite in 1893, *top pictures below*. This rigid, high-lift structure was demonstrated by Hargrave in London six years later and was adopted for the wings of many of the best European aeroplanes built before the 1914-18 War.

The lower illustration shows a replica of the Hawk glider built by Percy Pilcher in 1896. Having wheels, it could be towed into the air and made many fine flights of up to 250 yards. Within three years, Pilcher had designed a lightweight oil engine and was about to fit it to a new aircraft when he was killed in the Hawk. With him died Britain's chances of being the first country to produce a completely practical powered aeroplane.

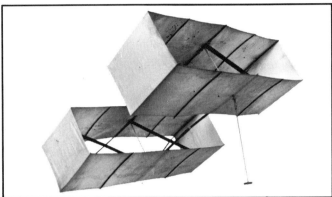

safely over long distances. However, we must not begrudge Herr Jatho his place in our story, as he certainly made some impressive hops in this contraption, covering up to 200 ft. in November 1903.

There was only one man alive who was destined to give the Wrights some real competition. This was Samuel Pierpont Langley, a famous astronomer and Secretary of the great Smithsonian Institution. As one would expect, he tackled the whole job scientifically and had enough money to test his ideas properly. Frail, flexible bird-shape wings like Ader's, and great lumbering barn-door structures like Maxim's failed to interest him.

Back in 1873-74, an Englishman named D.S. Brown had flown successfully a series of gliders with tandem wings. Langley allied their configuration with a 2-h.p. steam-engine in his 14-ft.-span model No. 5 of 1896, which he called an 'Aerodrome'. With its cambered wings, set at convincing angles of incidence and dihedral, two pusher propellers mounted between the wings, and cruciform tail, it looks as if it would fly, even to our modern eyes, accustomed to sleek streamlined metal monoplanes. And fly it did, covering up to 4,200 ft. at 25 m.p.h. on one occasion.

This achievement had interesting repercussions. Up to this time, would-be pilots and people who built aeroplanes had been considered slightly mad by the rest of the community. Balloons were one thing — gentle, quiet devices in which even ladies could be taken for a ride in their Sunday best, complete with picnic basket and a bottle or two of champagne. Aeroplanes were different. Even if they worked (which they didn't), they were dirty, noisy, smelly, beastly things of no particular sporting value.

It was difficult to continue feeling this way when so respectable and scientifically-minded a man as Professor Langley was tinkering with aeroplanes and, apparently, having some success with them. Even the U.S. Government felt it could no longer stand aloof, and when it found itself at war Spain in 1898, Langley was offered the money to build a full-size version of the 'Aerodrome', in the hope that it might have some military uses. Here was officialdom at its worst, already thinking how it might use for war a machine that had been the dream of men of goodwill for centuries — and doing so even before it had been perfected.

Langley felt, no doubt, that it was his duty to do as he was asked. In any case, it was good not to have to pay for the experiments himself any longer. It was at this stage that he made one of the great forward steps in flying history by building the first aircraft to fly successfully with a petrol-engine—the lightweight, high-power engine for which everyone had been waiting for so long. The aircraft was, admittedly, only a quarterscale model of the 'Aerodrome' he was building for the Government, but there seemed little reason why the full-size machine should be any less successful.

By October 7, 1903, all was ready for the first flight test. Being 69 years old, Langley had to ask somebody else to fly his aircraft; but the man who climbed into the open cockpit that autumn day was no mere hireling. Named Charles Manly, he was a fine engineer and had built the remarkable 52-h.p. five-cylinder radial engine with which the 'Aerodrome' was powered.

For some strange reason, it had been decided to launch the aircraft by catapult from the top of a houseboat on the Potomac River. It would have imposed less strain on the structure to let it take off on land, but perhaps the large clear expanse of river looked more attractive than even the biggest meadow, with trees and houses nearby. Certainly a scientist like Langley would not have believed that water might be a lot 'softer' to crash into than land!

Anyway, why think of crashing?

Already the engine was running noisily and he could see the structure of the 'Aerodrome' vibrating as the two pusher propellers made it strain at its leash. Suddenly, the catapult began to run forward, and a gasp of dismay went up from everyone present as the aircraft hit a post on the launching track and plunged into the river. Manly was unhurt and the aircraft was repairable; so it must have seemed like no more than an irritating setback that would soon be remedied. But what had Orville and Wilbur Wright been doing all this time?

As it happened, they too were just about ready to test their first powered aeroplane. So, if the public had been interested in such things (which they were not), they would have had an interesting race to follow—one that, ultimately, would have an immense influence on the future course of history and everyday life, for both good and evil.

It had taken the Wrights 4½ years of patient hard work, scientific study and sheer determination to get themselves to the starting line. Realising that the first essential was a control system that worked, they had begun in 1899 by building a biplane kite of 5 ft. span with which to test their ideas. Most important of these was the technique of controlling the direction of flight by warping (or twisting) the wingtips.

By means of control wires, they were able to warp the wingtips of their kite while it was in flight. The idea seemed to work, so they next built a full-size glider of 17 ft. span, which they took up to a place called Kill Devil Hills, near Kitty Hawk in North Carolina. Some writers claim the Wrights went there in order to keep their activities secret. In fact, it happened to be a place where they could hire a shed in which to work on their aircraft, where there was usually a nice steady breeze to help them into the air and plenty of soft sand if they came down quicker than planned.

Full-size glider No. 1 was flown mainly as a kite, although a few piloted flights were made at Kitty Hawk in October 1900. They returned in 1901 with glider No. 2 and in 1902

With both Lilienthal and Pilcher dead, Ader discouraged and Maxim no longer engaged in aeronautical experiments, Dr. S. P. Langley, an eminent astronomer and Secretary of the Smithsonian Institution, must have been regarded as the man most likely to succeed. In 1896, his 14-ft.-span steam-powered model aeroplane, *top left*, made a successful flight of well over three-quarters of a mile at 25 m.p.h., *lower picture*. Impressed, the U.S. War Department contributed $50,000 towards the cost of a full-size version. Langley called his machines 'Aerodromes'. Even to our modern eyes they look quite practical and he must have felt that he was on the brink of success as he prepared to launch the full-size machine from a house-boat on the Potomac River on October 7, 1903, *top right*. The pilot was Charles Manly, who was also responsible for the aircraft's remarkable 52-h.p. petrol engine.

First set-back to Langley's hopes came when the Aerodrome hit a post on the launching gear as it was catapulted from the houseboat, and plunged into the river. Undaunted, Langley and Manly set to work to repair it and were ready for a second attempt on December 8, 1903. This dramatic picture shows what happened: once again, the Aerodrome fell into the river after smashing its tail against the launching gear. Many years later, it was repaired, strengthened and modified by Glenn Curtiss, who flew it successfully as a seaplane; but by then powered flight had been an established fact for more than a decade.

The men who finally succeeded where so many others had failed were Wilbur and Orville Wright, brothers who ran a cycle shop in Dayton, Ohio. Key to their success is that they tackled the problem scientifically and painstakingly over a period of more than four years. As a start, they built a biplane kite of 5-ft. span to test in the air the wing-warping control system which they believed to be far superior to the body-movement technique used by Lilienthal. Having satisfied themselves that the system worked, they next embodied it in their 17-ft.-span No. 1 glider which was flown mainly as a kite, *top picture*. They added a front elevator control surface on No. 2 glider and a rudder on No. 3, *lower picture*, which spanned 32 ft. 1 in. and made many hundreds of successful piloted gliding flights in 1902-3. In the Summer of 1903, the Wrights began constructing a powered biplane on the same lines, but larger.

The simplicity of the Wright biplane belied the immense effort that went into its design and construction. When their No. 2 glider proved less efficient than expected, Wilbur and Orville built a wind tunnel, *lower right*, in which they tested dozens of different aerofoils before deciding which would be best for their powered biplane, *overleaf*, which they named the *Flyer*. Unable to buy a suitable engine, they made their own, *lower left*. Although less advanced than that in Langley's Aerodrome, it developed 12 h.p., which was adequate for an aircraft weighing only 750 lb. fully loaded. At 10.35 a.m. on December 17, 1903, with Orville at the controls, the *Flyer* left the ground for its first, brief 12-second flight. This historic moment in aviation history was captured on film by one of the five witnesses. The photograph that he took, *top*, shows Wilbur running by the wingtip as Orville struggles to keep the aircraft straight and level.

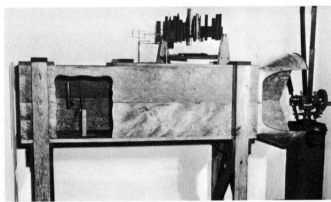

with glider No. 3. Between times, they tested dozens of tiny model wings in a wind-tunnel they had made at home from on old starch-box. They soon discovered that most of the published data on wing sections were wrong and devised new sections of their own. To their wing-warping control system they added first an elevator, stuck out in front of the wings, to make the aircraft climb and dive. Then they added a movable rudder behind the wings, for steering and to help keep the aircraft under control when the wings were warped.

When flying the gliders, they lay on the bottom wing with their hips in a little cradle which pulled the wing-warping wires when they swung their body to right or left—all very simple.

After making hundreds of flights in glider No. 3, Orville and Wilbur Wright decided they had learned enough to build a powered aeroplane. They still had to learn to build an engine and propeller to power it, but made an equally good job of this. Their 12-h.p. four-cylinder petrol-engine may not have been quite so good as Manly's radial, but it was good enough, and their propeller was superb. This was important, for if it had not been far more efficient than any built by earlier pioneers, it would never have lifted 750 lb. of aeroplane, fuel and pilot off the ground.

The Wrights had discovered the uselessness of trying to work out the size and shape of their propeller by the methods used by designers of ships' screws. Suddenly, they realised that an aircraft propeller works in much the same way as a wing—except that its 'lift' is forward instead of upward. So they made the blades of their propeller like small, cambered wings. This worked so well that they decided to fit two propellers driven—hardly surprisingly in view of their profession—by bicycle chains.

Engine and propellers were fitted to an improved version of their No. 3 glider, with a span of 40 ft. 4 in., and with this they set out once more for Kitty Hawk in the autumn of 1903. Still playing safe, they spent the first part of October brushing up their flying on the glider, remaining in the air for up to 43 seconds at a time. While doing so, they learned of the launching accident to Langley's 'Aerodrome' and must have realised that he would soon have the aircraft repaired and would try again.

Although the Wrights and Langley probably did not view it that way, the race was now on—as exciting as the present competition between America and Russia to be first to land a man on the Moon. Like the space race, this one had its share of setbacks.

When the Wrights tried to run their engine on the aircraft (confidently named the 'Flyer') it backfired and twisted one of the propeller shafts. Replacements did not arrive until November 20 and they also proved too weak. As Orville travelled impatiently back home, to make some

stronger shafts himself, he learned that Manly's second attempt to fly Langley's aeroplane, on December 8, had been no more successful than the first. Once again, the aircraft had hit against the launching gear and ended up in the river.

Only the newspapers found it amusing. One Boston journalist wrote: 'If Professor Langley had only thought to launch his air-ship bottom up, it would have gone into the air instead of down into the water.' Dreadfully disappointed, and with no more money to spare for such experiments, the old man gave up.

With their main competitor out of the running, the Wrights must have felt on the point of achieving their ambition on December 14, 1903, when the Flyer was prepared for its first flight. It had no wheels. Instead, its two launching skids were placed carefully on a small trolley, mounted on two bicycle hubs which ran along a wooden rail. They spun a coin to see who would try first, and Wilbur won; but it was not really his lucky day. Opening up to full throttle, he signalled for Orville to release the wire holding the aircraft back. Then, as it began trundling along the rail, he moved the front elevator to lift the Flyer into the air—too soon... the nose lifted briefly then smacked back into the sand. It was the end of flying for that day.

Not until December 17 were they ready to try again. This time it was Orville's turn to lie on the wing, his body inside the cradle which worked the wing-warping system and rudder, his left hand grasping the lever which controlled the elevator.

A handful of their friends from the nearby Life Saving Station had come along to watch; one of them was put in charge of a camera and told to click the shutter when he saw the Flyer leave the ground. The one and only photograph that he obtained must have appeared in more books than almost any other picture ever taken. It shows the aircraft in the air, and Wilbur running excitedly by one wingtip. What it does not show is the anxiety on Orville's face as he tried to keep the Flyer straight and level!

The big elevator was so powerful that the slightest movement of the hand-lever sent the machine climbing steeply to a height of about 10 feet. As soon as Orville tried to remedy this, the aircraft darted towards the ground. After 12 seconds of this switchback ride, a steeper dive than usual brought the Flyer back to earth with a bump— and so ended the first-ever powered, sustained and controlled (well, *nearly* controlled) flight in history.

Orville covered 120 feet, which is less than the wing span of a modern four-jet airliner; but, taking turns, the brothers flew three more times on that December day. Before damaging the elevator at the end of the last of these flights, Wilbur managed to stay in the air for 59 seconds, covering 852 feet. A few minutes later, the Flyer was overturned by a gust of wind and wrecked. But this did not matter; in a flying lifetime of 97 seconds it had proved conclusively that man could fly—not under a lighter-than-air 'bubble' carried by the wind, but in a machine with wings, that would one day climb, dive and wheel in the air like a bird at the touch of its pilot.

There were many differences between the way the Wrights tackled their experiments and the techniques of their greatest rival, Langley. As a start, being younger men, they were able to fly themselves, which made the whole business so much more exciting. Perhaps the greatest difference was in what it all cost. Langley spent nearly $50,000 on his launching gear alone, and it repaid him by wrecking his hopes. The Wrights calculated their expenditure at under $1,000, even including their railway fares to Kitty Hawk. For so small a sum, they changed the course of history.

THE GOLDEN YEARS

The newspapers of the world carried huge headlines on the day when the first men set foot on the Moon— and again three days later when the Apollo astronauts returned safely to Earth. How did the press react to the news that Orville and Wilbur Wright had made a hardly less momentous, if considerably shorter, hop in 1903? The answer is that it didn't! The few garbled reports that were published gave no hint of the size of the achievement.

If, therefore, the Wrights had stopped at that point, it is unlikely that they would be given a very prominent place in this book. In fact, they did not stop, but went home and began designing and building a better Flyer. They still did not fit it with wheels, which meant that after each flight it had to be hauled back to the starting point and put on to its launch-track before it could take off again. However, progress was rapid in other directions. In 1904 they invented a falling-weight catapult launch system which literally flung the aircraft into the air. Stability, control and power were all gradually improved, and by 1905 they were able to remain in the air for up to 38 minutes at a time.

Instead of having to go up to Kitty Hawk, they were able to fly these new aeroplanes from a place called the Huffman Prairie, only eight miles from their home in Dayton, Ohio. Unfortunately, their judgement was not always as good as their flying. This was apparent when, on May 25, 1904, they invited the whole of the local press to witness the first flight of Flyer No. 2 from their new airfield. They ought, at least, to have made one test hop first to ensure that the aircraft worked. But they didn't, and in front of all the assembled gentlemen of the press the aircraft simply ran off the end of the track and came to a halt. Wilbur and Orville knew why: the new engine was not giving its full power. When the press came again next day, the best the Flyer could manage was a glide of 60 feet. After this the editors were not interested even when passers-by claimed to have seen the Wrights making circuit after circuit of the Prairie 'in full flight'.

Who can really blame them? Even the U.S. Army, disappointed by its poor investment in the Langley machine, was not impressed when the Wrights offered to sell some of their aeroplanes for military reconnaissance duties. On October 24, 1905, a reply from the Board of Ordnance and Fortification said that the Army would not be interested 'until a machine is produced which by actual operation is shown to be able to produce horizontal flight and to carry an operator.' Nineteen days earlier, in its best flight of the year, Flyer No. 3 had flown just over 24 miles non-stop!

Once again, Wilbur and Orville made an error of judgement. They simply put away their aeroplane and did not fly again for nearly three years. Having learned to fly so well, at a time when nobody else had made even a properly controlled hop of a few yards, Wilbur wrote to a friend on October 10, 1906: 'We do not believe there is one chance in a hundred that anyone will have a machine of the least practical usefulness within five years.' The Wrights were never more wrong.

Over in France at that moment, the dapper little Brazilian airship-builder, Alberto Santos-Dumont, was putting the finishing touches to an aeroplane which he called the '14 bis'. It was a bent-looking tail-first contraption, with boxkite wings and tail based on Lawrence Hargrave's studies. Like the Wright Flyer, it had no seat. In this case, Santos-Dumont had to stand up, with the long fuselage and tail in front of him and the 50-h.p. engine behind him.

Weird as it was, the '14 bis' made history. On October 23, 1906, it flew nearly 200 feet and promptly won a prize of 3,000 francs for the first powered aeroplane to fly 25 metres (apparently the donor had not heard of the Wrights). On November 12 it improved its performance to 722 feet. This not only earned Santos-Dumont a further prize but, as the attempt was officially observed and timed, enabled him to set up the first-ever speed and distance records. His average speed worked out at a spanking 25.657 m.p.h.

Unlike the earlier exploits of the Wright brothers, these hops by Santos-Dumont caused a sensation. Here, at last, was proof that man could fly, complete with photographs. The fact that the '14 bis' was a pretty useless aeroplane was immaterial: the same was true of the Wright biplane, to a lesser extent, as aeroplanes with forward elevators

Even in 1908, five years after they became the first men to make sustained, controlled flights in a powered aeroplane, the Wrights were still unchallenged as the masters of flying. The upper photograph on this page reflects something of the confidence with which they flew their improved *Flyers* for up to 2 hr. 20 min. at a time. But the falling-weight catapult with which they launched their later aircraft, silhouetted in the foreground of the picture, symbolises the limitations of the Wright design.

By comparison with the Wright biplanes, Santos-Dumont's tail-first '14 bis', *lower picture*, was crude and clumsy. Its best flight, in 1906, covered a mere 722 ft.; but this marked the start of flying in Europe and better designs followed quickly.

Alberto Santos-Dumont, having achieved the satisfaction of flying in the '14 bis', *centre left*, started work immediately on designing the kind of aeroplane that would enable others to share his experience. The result was the tiny Demoiselle, two versions of which are shown in the top and bottom pictures on this page. With a structure of bamboo and canvas, the Demoiselle could be built at home by almost anybody, at a cost of about £ 300. When powered by a 25-h.p.

Darracq engine, it could fly at 60 m.p.h. — but there was a snag. Santos-Dumont, who can be seen standing in front of the aircraft in the top picture, weighed only eight stone. Heavier pilots often found that the little monoplane would not stagger off the ground under their weight. The 'do-it-yourself' design had, therefore, to give way gradually to professionally built machines like the Antoinette monoplane, *centre right*.

Few people regarded the aeroplane as a very practical vehicle until Louis Blériot made his historic cross-Channel flight on July 25, 1909. It mattered little that he would have had to ditch if a shower of rain had not cooled his overheating engine on the way, or that his monoplane was damaged in the heavy landing at Dover, *lower picture*.

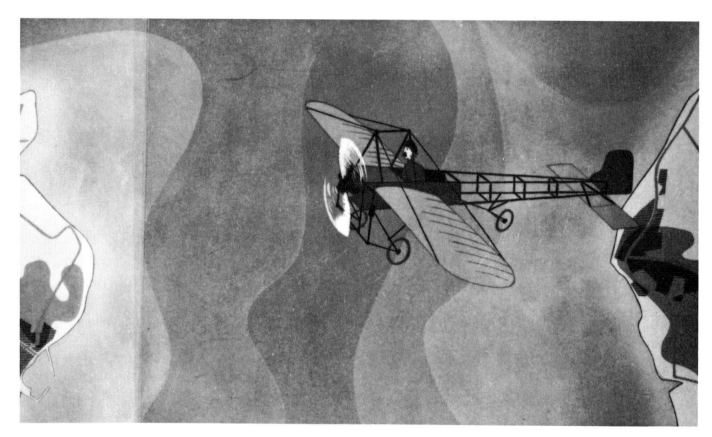

Madame Blériot was greeted triumphantly by her husband, *below*, when she followed by boat. If some of those who stood with Louis Blériot on the quayside at Dover looked forward to the time when they, too, might be able to fly between England and France, others already were beginning to ponder the significance of this aerial hop across the 'moat' that had been such an important part of Britain's defences.

were far less practical and efficient than the now familiar rear-tailed layout adopted by Cayley a century earlier, and used subsequently by people like Henson and du Temple.

The biggest technical contribution to flying made by the Wrights was their invention of the wing-warping control system, which foreshadowed the later use of ailerons. No less important was that their success, like that of Santos-Dumont, inspired others who designed and built far better aeroplanes.

Peak year for Wilbur and Orville was 1908. It began well, for in February they made their first aeroplane sale to the U.S. War Department, for $25,000. Of three aircraft ordered from different designers, it was the only one delivered and, therefore, able to try and meet the official requirement for a machine to carry two people for 125 miles at 40 m.p.h. A series of fine demonstration flights by Orville ended in tragedy on September 17, when one of the propellers broke, cutting a wire and causing the tail to collapse. The aircraft crashed from a height of 75 feet, injuring Orville and killing his passenger, Lt. T.E. Selfridge—first man to die in an accident to a powered aeroplane.

Undeterred by this mishap, the Army ordered an improved version which was accepted officially in the following year as 'Aeroplane No. 1, Heavier-than-air Division, United States aerial fleet.' From such a humble start sprang modern air power.

Meanwhile, Wilbur had been doing great things in France, which had become the world centre of flying. Unlike America, where nobody was interested, and Britain, where our greatest pioneer, A.V. Roe, was issued with a summons as a public menace (one charge being that he kept the local tramps awake with the noise of his aero-engines), France welcomed people who wanted to fly. The men who congregated there were as colourful as the cast of the film of *Those Magnificent Men in their Flying Machines*. We remember them today as the great pilots of aviation's golden years, from 1903 to 1914.

First among them was Santos-Dumont who, after abandoning the big and clumsy '14 bis', went to the other extreme and built such a dainty little machine that it was christened the 'Demoiselle'. His idea was to design such a simple aeroplane that anyone could build and fly it at home. The fuselage was made of bamboo poles; the ings spanned only 16½ feet, and the whole thing weighed a mere 243 lb. without the pilot, who sat level with the wheels, under the wings.

Then there was Louis Blériot, with the droopy moustache, whose automobile-lamp manufacturing firm made just enough money to pay for his attempts to fly. At a time when everyone crashed occasionally, he did it so regularly that he acquired a reputation as the aviator most likely to kill himself. He never did so, but he did make the first aero-

By 1909 aviation was already becoming an industry in Europe. First to begin manufacturing aeroplanes for other people were the Voisin brothers in France. Henry Farman used one of their boxkite biplanes, *below*, *top*, to win the Deutsch Archdeacon prize for the first circular flight of more than one kilometre in Europe, on January 13, 1908. In Britain, the Short brothers supplemented their balloon construction with the manufacture of six Wright biplanes under licence. The first of these Short-built Wrights was bought by the Hon. C.S. Rolls, co-founder of the Rolls-Royce company with Sir Henry Royce. In the lower picture on this page, Rolls is shown seated between Horace Short and Orville Wright in the front of a Rolls-Royce car, with Wilbur Wright, bowler-hatted like his brother, on the back seat.

The rapid progress made by aviation in the decade before the 1914-18 War was made possible by the steadily-increased power and efficiency of contemporary aero-engines. Most famous of them was the Gnome rotary, in which the crankshaft was bolted rigidly to the aircraft structure, while the cylinders rotated round it, as shown in the upper illustrations on this page. The seven-cylinder Gnome of 1909 rotated at 1,200 r.p.m., developed 50 h.p. and weighed 165 lb.

Aero shows were held in Paris and London at which the new industry could display its wares. Exhibits in the first British Aero Show, at Olympia in 1909, included airships, kites and a partially-completed biplane of Short Brothers design. However, all the really practical aeroplanes were of French origin.

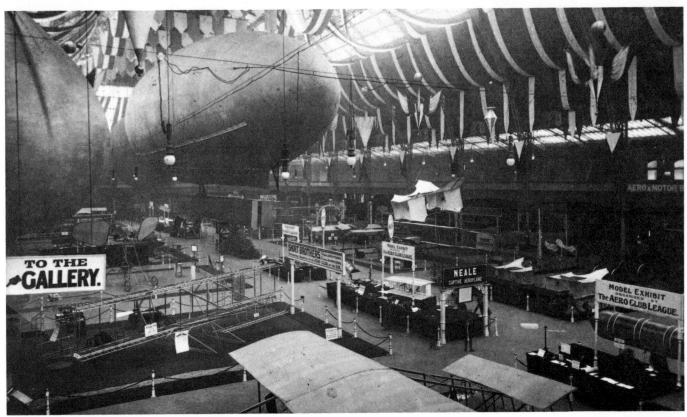

Before he became world famous by flying across the Channel, Louis Blériot was best-known for his spectacular crashes. The upper picture on this page shows all that was left of the 50-h.p. Blériot XII monoplane after his accident at Rheims on August 29, 1909. As usual, he escaped without serious injury. He also had the satisfaction of winning a 10,000-franc prize for the highest speed over 10 km. achieved during the Rheims Aviation Meeting, by averaging 47.75 m.p.h. in this aircraft before the crash.

The five years from 1909 to 1914 were the golden age of International flying meetings. Star performers included Henry Farman, who was by now a constructor as well as a pilot. The Farman biplane, *lower pictures*, was an improved version of the Voisin, powered usually by a Gnome or Vivinus engine of 50 h.p. Top speed was only 37 m.p.h.; but there was plenty of excitement when pilots like Farman (aircraft No. 30) and Sommer (No. 6) matched their courage and skill by racing around the pylons at Rheims.

Progress in England was slower than in France, as both the authorities and the public tended to regard aeroplanes and pilots as a nuisance. Among the pioneers who refused to be discouraged by this attitude was Horatio Phillips. The bizarre appearance of his 'Venetian blind' aircraft caused them to be regarded as freaks. In fact, Phillips' research into cambered double-surface aerofoils made a great contribution to aviation progress and every 'slat' on his aircraft was a narrow-chord wing. He progressed from an unpiloted version, tested successfully at Harrow in 1893, to

the 'single-blind' piloted multiplane of 1904, *upper picture*, which did not fly, and another with four 'blinds' which, in 1907, became the first powered aeroplane to fly in Britain.

Much more practical were the designs of A. V. Roe, Britain's greatest pioneer of the early 20th century. The lower photograph shows the aircraft in which he made his first hops, in June 1908, being removed from its shed at Brooklands.

plane flight over the English Channel on July 25, 1909, in an aeroplane of his own design, earning a prize of £1,000 from the *Daily Mail* newspaper and £3,000 from the French government. He did it, incidentally, with one foot swated in bandages, after a crash.

Santos-Dumont, the Wrights and Blériot were one-man, or two-brother, teams, designing, building and flying their own aeroplanes. A few professional plane-builders began to appear on the scene at this time—men like the Voisin brothers in France, and the Short brothers in England, who were more interested in building good machines for other people than in flying themselves. And, of course, there were the first professional pilots—men who began, at least, by testing and flying the products of others.

Typical was bearded Henry Farman, son of an English journalist, but living in France and speaking French. On January 13, 1908, he won a 50,000-franc prize for making the first circular flight of more than one kilometre in Europe, on a Voisin biplane, and this marked the start of really practical flying in Europe.

Another was Hubert Latham, who decided he might just as well live dangerously and learn to fly when his doctors told him he had only one year to live. In fact, after winning countless prizes at flying meetings and nearly beating Blériot across the Channel, he died on safari in Africa as the victim of a wounded buffalo.

Such were the characters of the golden years of flying. Aviation had not yet become a great industry and aeroplanes had not acquired guns and bombs and learned to kill, although both developments were being planned. Instead, aviators learned to fly by sitting in the cockpit, opening up the engine, taxiing over the bumpy grass a few times and then taking off on their first solo, which was often, simultaneously, the first test flight of their aircraft. Except in the case of a major structural failure, such as the wings coming off in flight, even crashes were seldom serious. Aeroplanes were so lightly made, of wood, wire and canvas, that they crumpled up in an accident, absorbing most of the impact.

This was the circus-like scene in which Wilbur Wright found himself when he set up camp near Le Mans. The light-hearted way in which some of the Europeans seemed to be taking their flying must have appalled him. With the proper dignity one would expect from the sons of a bishop, the Wrights flew in immaculate suits, complete with collar and tie, relaxing only far enough to turn their cap back to front sometimes. At least one of their passengers sat on the leading-edge of the Flyer's bottom wing wearing a bowler hat. With the propellers spinning only a few feet behind him, one hopes that it was jammed firmly in place.

There is little doubt of the respect with which other pilots regarded the Wrights. They flocked to Wilbur's camp to watch him working and flying. A. V. Roe even cycled

CONQUEST OF THE AIR, 1874-1914 The pictures on this and the opposite page symbolise four of the major stages in the evolution of the aeroplane, from the first shaky hops to the time when the aeroplane was sufficiently advanced to be put to work.

No contemporary drawings give so good an impression of the probable appearance of du Temple's aeroplane of 1874 as does the model, *upper picture*, which forms part of the Qantas collection. Lack of a suitable lightweight engine, which plagued du Temple and others, did not deter Otto Lilienthal, *lower picture*, whose epic gliding flights in 1890-96 proved that heavier-than-air flight was entirely practicable.

Inspired by Lilienthal, encouraged by Chanute and confident of their own ability, Orville and Wilbur Wright also benefited, more than anything, from the invention of the petrol engine. The power to fly was at last available and it enabled the Wright *Flyer* (*top picture*) to make the first-ever powered, sustained and controlled flights by a heavier-than-air machine on December 17, 1903.

Of what use was the aeroplane? In the first decade after the Wright brothers' achievement, the answer seemed to be that it could provide sport and spectacle. A few people expected it to be of some value for military reconnaissance. It is doubtful if anyone would have expected to see pre-1914 aircraft still providing a spectacle in the mid-1960s; yet the Eardley Billing biplane replica, *lower picture*, was only one of the stars of the film *Those Magnificent Men in their Flying Machines*.

In order to save sufficient money for his experiments, A.V. Roe, *top picture*, lived on five shillings' worth of food each week. The enforced simplicity of his designs contributed greatly to their success. More elaborate but less successful was Lt. J. W. Seddon's aeroplane, *centre*, which contained more than a mile of metal tubing; named *Mayfly*, it didn't! However, it achieved modest fame as the largest aeroplane in the world up to that time, with 1,000 sq. ft. of wing surface, two 65-h.p. engines and an unloaded weight of about 2,600 lb.

France remained the centre of world aviation in these pre-war years — a fact underlined by the bottom picture on this page. Taken at the first international air race held at Hendon, on September 25, 1913, it shows Claude Grahame-White's Maurice Farman biplane flying over a Blériot and two Morane-Saulnier monoplanes, all of French design.

First to fly, officially, in Britain was American-born S.F. Cody. A natural showman, he did not let his appointment as Instructor in Kiting to the British Army deter him from wearing 'Wild West' clothes and riding around on a richly-saddled white horse, *top right*. But showmanship was allied with courage and engineering ability, and the combination of these qualities enabled him to fly 1,390 ft. in his British Army Aeroplane No. 1, *top left*, over Laffan's Plain, Farnborough, on October 16, 1908. By 1912 he had developed the design into the Cody military biplane, *centre left*, in which he won the government-sponsored military trials, staged on Salisbury Plain. The idea of the trials was to find the best aircraft with which to equip the newly-formed Royal Flying Corps. Despite its success, the Cody machine was certainly not suited for this job and the R.F.C. flew mainly the products of the French aircraft industry and its own Royal Aircraft Factory at Farnborough. From the start Farnborough was also an important research centre. In the bottom picture, taken there in 1912, the strength of the wings of a Bristol Coanda monoplane is being tested by loading them with sandbags.

FROM WAR TO PEACE, 1918-19 One of the greatest fighting aircraft of the 1914-18 War was Germany's Fokker D. VII biplane, shown in the upper illustration on this page. Designed by a team formed by Anthony Fokker, a Dutchman, it achieved many successes in the final months of the War. This particular example, rebuilt by Cole Palen in America, is still airworthy.

Also still to be seen is the Vickers Vimy illustrated on the opposite page. Designed as a bomber, but too late to take part in the 1914-18 War, this particular Vimy was used by Alcock and Brown for the first non-stop flight across the Atlantic on June 14-15, 1919. Now in London's Science Museum, its fuselage is left uncovered to show the extra fuel tanks installed for the flight. The smaller picture below shows a replica of the Vimy's cockpit which is displayed separately, emphasising how few instruments and navigation aids the two airmen had to help them on their way.

While richer men were able to purchase their aeroplanes in France, A.V. Roe had to continue building his own. As the only engine he could afford developed a mere 9 h.p., he built the tiny 20-ft.-span triplane shown below and covered it with brown paper. In this aircraft, on July 13, 1909, he became, officially, the first British pilot to fly an all-British aeroplane, by covering about 100 ft. at Lea Marshes. Ten days later, he flew 900 ft. in the same machine.

To fly before the 1914-18 War was a tremendous adventure. The draughtiness of her perch does not seem to be worrying the demure young lady seen preparing for a flight with Claude Grahame-White in this photograph, taken during the meeting at Blackpool in 1910.

there, being unable to afford any other means of transport after paying his boat fare across the Channel. They were not disappointed with what they saw. During the second half of 1908, Wilbur carried dozens of passengers, flew solo for up to 2 hours 20 minutes at a time without landing, and started a modest flying school. Even the crowned heads of Europe, including King Edward VII, went to see the modern miracle of a man who flew confidently and well.

No other aeroplane in the world could approach the performance of the Wright biplane at this time, but it was nearing the end of its period of leadership. Humble as they felt in the presence of such mastery of the air, men like Blériot and A. V. Roe still felt that their propeller-at-the-front, tail-at-the-rear designs would ultimately be better, and they were right.

Front-elevator machines were still to enjoy a few years of success, particularly in the improved forms evolved by men like Farman. Wheeled undercarriages freed such aircraft from the shackles of catapult launching. Most important of all, a French engineer named Seguin invented an incredible new lightweight engine which he called the Gnome. It was a 'rotary' engine, in which the crankshaft remained stationary, bolted to the aircraft, while the cylinders rotated with the propeller. This may seem an odd way of doing things, but it saved weight and improved cooling, and those who began by regarding it as a freak soon admitted that it was one of the keys to further progress in the air.

Previously, when a new aeroplane had been ready to attempt its first take-off, it was usual for the pilot's friends to lie flat on the ground, watching excitedly for the slightest glimmer of daylight between the wheels and the grass. When fitted with the 50 h.p. Gnome, aircraft like the British Bristol Boxkite climbed to 150 feet without difficulty, even on their first flight. Nobody went much higher than that, as aeroplanes were not fitted with instruments and if a pilot had entered cloud he would have had only instinct and a sense of balance—neither of them reliable—to tell him whether or not he was still flying straight and level.

With the basic problems of flying now solved, progress was rapid. The first aero exhibition was staged in the centre

of Paris in 1908, and no fewer than a quarter of a million people went to Rheims in August 1909 to watch most of the world's leading pilots compete in the first-ever air races. They had their money's worth, for records were broken almost every day. Nobody was killed, although one Voisin was wrecked and Blériot had yet another serious accident in his 50-h.p. monoplane after breaking the speed record. This only added to the excitement, and soon flying meetings were being held everywhere, even in Britain.

Because of official and public disinterest, flying on this side of the Channel still trailed behind that in France. The first powered flight by an Englishman seems to have been made by Horatio Phillips in the summer of 1907, when he covered some 500 feet in what looked like a Venetian blind fitted with wheels and a propeller. A. V. Roe was next, on June 8, 1908, with sizeable hops in a tail-first biplane at Brooklands; but the first official flights in Britain were made by Samuel Franklin Cody, one of aviation's most colourful figures, on October 16, 1908.

Cody was American-born, although he became a naturalised Briton in 1909. Like his famous namesake, 'Buffalo Bill' Cody, he sported a goatee beard and had fought Indians as a scout in earlier years, before touring with his own Wild West show.

Flying presented the kind of challenge and adventure that attracted Cody. He began by building man-lifting

Even in a stick-and-string era, some designers were already beginning to appreciate the importance of reducing drag to a minimum. Henri Fabre, in France, invented a unique wooden lattice-girder spar, which was as strong as the usual box spar but allowed the airflow to pass between the top and bottom flanges. He used this form of construction in the aeroplane he built for pioneer pilot Louis Paulhan, *upper picture*, in 1911. The streamlined cockpit nacelle was another innovation.

Paulhan's usual mount at that time was a Farman biplane and he is best remembered as the winner of a £10,000 *Daily Mail* prize, earned in this type of aircraft, for the first flight between London and Manchester in under 24 hours. In an effort to beat his French rival, *bottom picture*, Claude Grahame-White made the first-ever night flight, but even this was not enough to reduce Paulhan's lead.

kites, which seemed so much better than observation balloons that he was appointed Instructor in Kiting to the British Army. Regular officers tended to become apoplectic when they saw him riding around official establishments on a richly-saddled white horse, with his long hair flowing beneath a large stetson and with a pearl-handled revolver dangling from his belt. But there was no doubt of the man's courage and ability.

With funds provided by the government, he built the Army's first aeroplane and then flew it 1,390 feet at a height of 50-60 feet over Laffan's Plain, Farnborough, where the great air shows are held today. Like Cody himself, the aeroplane was huge and rugged, and was known usually as the 'Cathedral'. It was even more of a dead-end design than the Wright biplane but, allied to Cody's showmanship, went a long way towards making the people of Britain airminded.

The first officially-recognised flight by a British pilot in the United Kingdom was made by J. T. C. Moore-Brabazon (later Lord Brabazon) in a French Voisin on May 2, 1909; but the real start of British flying was on July 13, 1909, when A. V. Roe made the first completely satisfactory—if short—flight in an all-British aeroplane. The tiny triplane that he built and flew can still be seen in the Science Museum, London, its wings and fuselage covered with brown paper in an effort to make it light enough to leave the ground even though its JAP engine developed only 9 h.p. Roe could not afford a better engine, and had to live on five shillings' worth of food each week to save enough cash even for this modest machine.

On the whole, flying continued to be regarded as a sport in the years that were left before the world was plunged into war in August 1914. Nobody made much money from it, but it was real, personal flying—the kind that men had always dreamed about. Nobody was yet quite sure of the best design for an aeroplane. Biplanes and monoplanes, with engines both at the front and behind the wings, all performed equally well at the low speeds made possible by engines of the period. Other shapes, too, were being tried out. The first primitive helicopters had left the ground in France in 1907. The first seaplane had followed, also in France, on March 28, 1910; but it was left to the brilliant designer-pilot Glenn Curtiss, greatest U.S. pioneer after the Wrights, to produce the first really practical seaplanes and flying-boats in 1911-12.

The possibility that flying might one day perform a useful service for the man in the street was suggested by the first experimental air mail services in 1911, first in India and then in Britain, where 100,000 letters and cards were flown between Hendon and Windsor to mark the coronation of King George V. But there were more sinister developments as well.

In France, a Voisin biplane shown at the 1911 Aero Show

had a formidable-looking gun mounted on its nose. Another French aeroplane built that year was armoured to protect its crew against ground fire in battle. In fact, it was even safer than its designers had planned, being so heavy that it would fly only a few yards.

In America, Curtiss biplanes made the first landing and take-off from a wooden deck on a warship, foreshadowing the aircraft carrier of the future. Governments began spending more and more money on military aeroplanes and airships, although they saw no use for such machines except as 'aerial cavalry' for reconnaissance. Neverthless, experiments in fitting guns, bombs and even torpedoes for more warlike duties continued.

The public did not take such developments seriously. For them flying was synonymous with racing, with stunts like flying through Tower Bridge, London, and linking for the first time by air cities such as London and Manchester, and London and Paris. When the first aerobatics were added to the repertoire at flying meetings, they became even more excited and even more convinced that flying was only for supermen, and a handful of superwomen.

Unknown to anyone was that the first man to loop the loop—the Russian pilot Nesterov—was to be the first of his country's airmen to die in action in the great war that was about to give the aeroplane a real job to do for the first time.

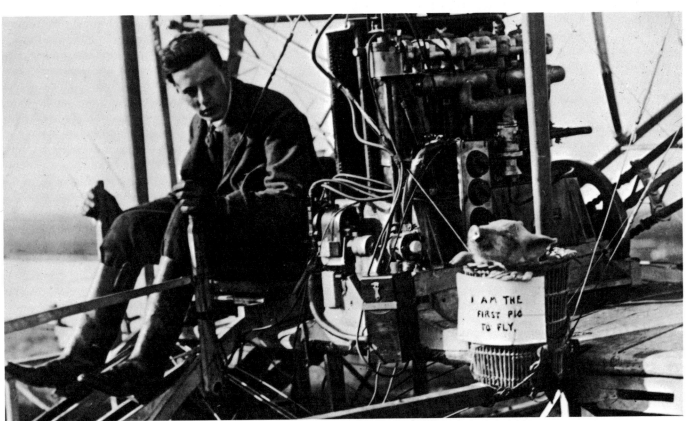

FROM DREAM
TO NIGHTMARE

When the First World War began on August 4, 1914, few of the generals and admirals in command of combat units expected aeroplanes to be of the slightest help to them. It was possible that these new-fangled flying machines might make an occasional reconnaissance flight, given the right kind of weather; but only Germany's huge Zeppelin airships looked powerful enough and impressive enough for worthwhile jobs like keeping track of fleet movements in the North Sea and bomb-dropping.

There was some excuse for scepticism. When the Royal Flying Corps sent its four first-line Squadrons to France in the first month of the war, it was able to muster a total of only 105 officers, 63 aeroplanes and 95 motor vehicles. The only armament carried by the aircraft consisted of the pilot's personal revolver, plus the odd carbine or sporting rifle stowed in the observer's cockpit. The ground transport was no more convincing to a professional soldier. One lorry, intended to carry high explosives for No. 5 Squadron, had been taken over hurriedly from a famous sauce manufacturer and remained bright scarlet with *The World's Appetiser* printed in large gold letters on each side.

Germany had the largest air force, with 260 aircraft in front-line service. The French air force was a little smaller, but had behind it the finest aircraft industry in the world, capable not only of meeting the needs of its own fighting forces but of supplying hundreds of excellent machines to Britain and its other allies. This was important because the British government had no more idea of how to build up a strong air force in 1912-14 than it has today.

When the Royal Flying Corps had been formed in 1912, it was divided into Military and Naval Wings. The War Office made it clear that it intended to equip the Military Wing exclusively with aeroplanes designed in its 'nationalised' Royal Aircraft Factory at Farnborough. This seemed a fairly safe policy at the time, as one of the best aeroplanes in the country was undoubtedly the B.E.2 designed at Farnborough by a young man named Geoffrey de Havilland. By the time it had been developed into the B.E.2C version, it was so rock-steady in flight that it was difficult to imagine a better reconnaissance aircraft. Unfortunately, as we shall see later, this apparently desirable quality was to prove disastrous in action, and lead in 1916 to the decision to switch to aeroplanes built by Britain's private industry.

There might have been no industry to turn to for help had not the Admiralty, under Winston Churchill, decided from the start to equip the Naval Wing of the R.F.C. with the best machines available, wherever they came from.

In some other respects, the Navy was as short-sighted as the War Office. Fearing that it might lose too many of its more adventurous young officers to the Naval Wing, it emphasised that their career would suffer if they were misguided enough to want to fly. In particular, they would not be able to take command of one of His Majesty's ships, however senior their rank.

Those who volunteered to fly under such circumstances could hardly fail to become enthusiastic pilots, although enthusiasm did not always imply aptitude for the job. For example, one naval captain broke up five training 'planes in four days. When he was sent up for his final test, in an effort to get him back to sea in the shortest possible time, the three judges sought refuge in a hangar and watched his performance through an open door. Unable to stand the strain again, they told him he had passed and asked him to fly his machine back to the other side of the airfield. In doing so, he broke off the undercarriage, setting up a record of destruction that may never have been beaten.

On the whole, pilots of the Royal Flying Corps and Royal Naval Air Service (which grew out of the Naval Wing in July 1914) were of much higher standard than that particular Captain. They needed to be, as the aeroplanes of 1914 had all kinds of little tricks. Nobody yet knew how to recover from a spin; but if one of the Maurice Farman 'Longhorn' trainers used by the R.F.C. entered too steep a dive the remedy was simple. The pilot only had to steepen the dive beyond the vertical, fly upside down and hope the wings would stay on. The real problem arose if he was too close to the ground for such drastic action, as no British pilots had parachutes in the first World War. Apparently, someone in a high place felt that if a pilot had a parachute, he might be tempted to abandon an aircraft which, although

Among the designers at the Royal Aircraft Factory before the 1914-18 War was a young man named Geoffrey de Havilland. His B.E. 2 biplane, having been built at the Factory, was not allowed to compete against the products of private manufacturers in the 1912 military trials. However, it completed some tests unofficially and showed that it could beat all comers in the important speed-range and climb tests. From it was developed the B.E.2A, *top left*, with 70-h.p. Renault engine. This aircraft went into large-scale production for the R.F.C., equipping both operational squadrons and training units at the Central Flying School, *top right*.

Fastest aeroplane of its day was the streamlined Deperdussin monoplane, *lower picture*, which was powered by a 160-h.p. Gnome engine. Piloted by Maurice Prévost, it became the first aircraft to fly 200 km. (124 miles) in an hour on September 29, 1913.

The Maurice Farman S. 7 biplane illustrated below was privately-owned and used for racing; but similar aircraft served as trainers with both the Royal Flying Corps and the Royal Naval Air Service. The French air force continued to use them for reconnaissance until May 1915, when they were replaced by the improved Maurice Farman S.11.

First reconnaissance flights, *right,* made by the R.F.C. in France, on August 19, 1914, were flown by Captain (later Air Chief Marshal Sir) Philip Joubert de la Ferté in a Blériot XI monoplane and Lt. Gilbert

Mapplebeck in a B.E. 2B. Reconnaissance remained a primary duty of the air forces throughout the 1914-18 War, proving of inestimable value to the army commanders. Standard reconnaissance machine in the later stages of the war was the Factory-designed R.E.8, *bottom left,* of which 4,077 were built, with a 150-h.p. R.A.F. 4a engine and armament of two machine-guns. The first fighters were Morane-Saulnier monoplanes, *bottom right,* fitted with a forward-firing machine-gun and with steel deflector plates on the propeller to kick aside bullets that would otherwise have hit the blades.

damaged, was still capable of being landed in one piece. Whether or not this was the primary reason, the absence of parachutes cost the lives of many fine pilots who might have been able to bale out of a flaming aircraft, at a time when a fighter like the Sopwith Pup cost a mere £710.18s., plus a further £620 for its engine.

This lack of a parachute must have been in the minds of the pilots of Nos. 2, 3, 4 and 5 Squadrons when they flew their motley assortment of aeroplanes across the Channel in August 1914, as they had just one warlike assignment —to ram any Zeppelin they might spot on the way! However, they were well prepared for other eventualities, as each pilot wore a motor car inner tube round his body as a makeshift life-belt, and carried in his aircraft a pair of field glass, spare goggles, a roll of tools, a water bottle containing boiled water, a small stove and a haversack containing biscuits, cold meat, chocolate and a packet of soup-mix.

In this manner, Britain's first air force flew into action, and it was not long before army commanders began to change their minds about its value. The German armies had advanced as far as the River Marne. If they had not been held, the war might have ended in a matter of weeks, with the Germans in Paris; but they were held. When the immediate danger was over, the British Commander-in-Chief, Field-Marshal Sir John French, wrote in his dispatch:

'I wish particularly to bring to your notice the admirable work done by the Royal Flying Corps under Sir David Henderson. Their skill, energy and perseverance have been beyond all praise. They have furnished me with the most complete and accurate information, which has been of incalculable value in the conduct of operations. Fired at constantly both by friend and foe, and not hesitating to fly in every kind of weather, they have remained undaunted throughout. Further, by actually fighting in the air, they have succeeded in destroying five of the enemy's machines.'

One thing that has not changed in all the years of air warfare is the probability of being shot at by friend and foe. Armies and navies, having suffered much from air attack tend, on spotting an aircraft, to shoot first and ask questions afterwards, and many lives have been lost needlessly. To reduce such wastage, aircraft began to carry national markings after a time. British aeroplanes had large Union Jacks painted on their wings and fuselage: French machines acquired the familiar blue, white and red roundels, German aircraft a black cross. Before long, the R.F.C. and R.N.A.S. switched to copies of the French insignia, with the colours reversed. But the real answer was to teach aircraft recognition — an art which has always seemed beyond the grasp of anti-aircraft gunners.

The five enemy aircraft mentioned by Sir John French were brought down in various ways. On one occasion, hav-

The upper painting shows a dog-fight of 1918, with the crew of a
D.H.9 day-bomber trying desperately to beat off an attack by five
German Albatros D. V. fighters.

The 'Fokker Scourge' began when Anthony Fokker evolved for his
Type E monoplanes a proper interrupter gear which 'timed' the
bullets from a machine-gun to pass between the blades of a propeller.
Flown by men like Max Immelmann, seen in action in the lower picture
opposite, the Fokkers almost shot the Allied air forces from
the sky in 1915. Yet, surprisingly, no more than about 400 were
built. Max. speed of the Fokker E. III monoplane, with 100-h.p.
Oberursel engine, was 87 m.p.h.

ing run out of revolver bullets, the British pilot performed such dangerous manoeuvres a few inches above the German pilot's head that the latter was only too happy to make a safe forced landing and surrender. An advantage of the light, slow-flying aircraft of 1914 was that they could be landed almost anywhere; on this occasion the British crew were able to taxi up to the enemy machine and take over their prisoners personally.

Now that the tremendous value of air reconnaissance for keeping track of enemy troop movements was fully proven, this continued to be a primary task of the air forces in France, and wherever else armies fought. Techniques were gradually improved, first by the use of photography to supplement visual reports, and then by using radio to pass messages to the ground instead of making signals or having to land. An allied task was to circle over the battlefield spotting where the shells from friendly artillery were falling, and correcting the aim of the gunners to ensure maximum discomfort for the enemy.

Unlike soldiers in the muddy trenches below, the airmen engaged in these operations found it difficult to regard their opponents with much hostility. They took occasional pot-shots at each other because this was expected of them; but it was a man-to-man affair, rather like knights in shining armour at an ancient tourney. If somebody got hurt, it was rather a shame, but all part of the game. Having used up all their ammunition, it was not unusual for Allied and German airmen to fly alongside each other and wave a cheery farewell.

Even when the war reached its full fury, and airmen on both sides were dying by the hundred, something of this spirit remained. If a particularly respected foe was shot down, it was usual to drop a message to his colleagues at the enemy airfield, telling what had happened, and promising a funeral with full military honours and a safe passage at a certain time if they liked to fly over and drop a wreath. All of which the soldiers engaged in a dirtier kind of war found difficult to understand.

Air fighting grew out of the need to prevent enemy reconnaissance aircraft from doing their job and to protect one's own reconnaissance machines. Clearly, this called for the use of machine-guns: the problem was to fit them in a way that would make them effective.

It was realised from the start that the ideal fighter would be a small, fast single-seater with a tractor propeller (i.e., propeller at the front). Unfortunately, if one fitted a machine-gun to the fuselage of such an aircraft, and opened fire, the results were suicidal, as the bullets simply chewed away the propeller spinning a few feet in front of the gun. Some successes were achieved by mounting the gun at an angle, so that the bullets passed outside the propeller 'disc'; but this meant that the pilot flew in one direction and fired in another, requiring far more luck than judgement.

The first fighters were, therefore, two-seaters—usually with a 'pusher' engine behind the wings and the observer/gunner in the nose, forward of the pilot. This worked, except that such aircraft tended to be slower and more cumbersome than the reconnaissance machines they were supposed to catch and shoot down.

Knowing all this, the observer of a German aeroplane cruising over the trenches on April 1, 1915 did not worry very much when he saw a French Morane-Saulnier single-seat tractor monoplane flying straight towards him. He might just have had time to be startled and frightened as a hail of machine-gun bullets passed miraculously through the propeller disc of the Morane and sent his machine crashing to the ground. Certainly, he was unable to warn any of his friends of what had happened, and two more German aircraft were lost in equally mysterious circumstances on April 13 and 18.

On the following day, the Morane force-landed on the wrong side of the lines and its secret was revealed.

Pilot of the Morane was none other than Roland Garros, the famous sporting pilot who, among other pre-war achievements, had made the first flight across the Mediterranean on September 23, 1913. After spending a period at the Morane works, helping Raymond Saulnier to devise a way of firing a machine-gun straight ahead from a tractor monoplane, he returned to his unit with the rather crude answer. It consisted of fitting steel deflector plates to the propeller blades, to kick aside any bullets that would have hit the blades when the machine-gun, mounted forward of the cockpit, was fired. Sufficient bullets passed between the blades to make the idea practical, as Garros quickly proved.

Anthony Fokker, the Dutch pioneer who built many of the best aircraft of the war for Germany, was told to copy the idea. Instead of taking this easy course, he worked with two of his designers, named Leinberger and Lübbe, to perfect an interrupter gear that would 'time' the bullets from a machine-gun to pass between the propeller blades. He fitted it to his little monoplane fighters which, flown by men like Max Immelmann and Oswald Boelcke, soon began shooting the Allied air forces from the sky.

The B.E.2C's of the Royal Flying Corps were sitting ducks for the Fokkers. Because of their superb stability, which made them ideal for reconnaissance, they were not manoeuvrable enough to out-fly the enemy single-seaters. Nor could they defend themselves, for the observer/gunner sat in the front cockpit and was so surrounded by wings, wires and struts that he could seldom get a clear shot at his attacker. Things grew so bad that on one occasion a lone B.E.2C was scheduled to have an escort of no fewer than 12 other aircraft in an effort to protect it during a reconnaissance flight.

The 'Fokker Scourge' lasted from October 1915 until

Most of the great British fighter aces flew S.E.5s and 5As in 1917-18. Those illustrated below equipped No. 85 Squadron of the R.A.F. in France. With a 200-h.p. Hispano or Wolseley Viper engine, they had a top speed of 138 m.p.h. and were armed with two machine-guns.

From the start, in April 1918, the newly-formed Royal Air Force placed great emphasis on strategic bombing. The top right illustration on this page shows the largest and smallest bombs dropped on Germany in the closing months of the War. Beneath it is shown a replica of the blood-red Fokker Triplane that was the favourite mount of Germany's ace of aces, Baron Manfred von Richthofen, who claimed 80 victories in aerial combat over the Western Front in France.

May of the following year, when Anthony Fokker's monoplane at last met its match in the British D.H.2 and F.E.2B 'pusher' fighters and the little French Nieuport tractor biplane. The Nieuport carried its gun above the top wing, firing outside the propeller disc; but before long Allied fighters, too, had interrupter gears, and a succession of magnificent machines such as the British Pup, Camel and S.E.5A and French Spads and Nieuports ensured that the German air force never again ruled the skies.

First one side then the other gained brief leadership, as new and better aircraft appeared. The rôle of the fighters did not change; but while defending their own two-seaters and attacking those of the enemy, they often ran into squadrons of enemy fighters doing the same job in reverse. Then there would be a furious 'dog-fight', with perhaps dozens of aircraft chasing each other, and the staccato rattle of machine-gun fire followed by brilliant bursts of orange and yellow flame as a crippled aircraft span slowly out of the melée or dived faster and faster until its wings broke away and it slammed into 'no-man's land.'

From such fighting emerged the 'aces' — men like Mannock and McCudden of the R.F.C., Bishop and Collishaw from Canada, Guynemer and Fonck of France, Coppens of Belgium, von Richthofen and Udet of Germany — who scored victory after victory in aerial combat. Looking today at the survivors of the aircraft they flew, it seems incredible

that such tiny, dainty, wood and canvas biplanes, powered by engines no more powerful than those fitted in modern lightplanes, could have dealt out death and destruction on a vast scale; yet the nine pilots listed above alone claimed a total of 570 aircraft shot down in aerial combat.

The German pilots, in particular, painted their aircraft in bright colours and patterns. Von Richthofen's Fokker Triplane was a vivid scarlet, making it easy for troops down below to identify the 'Red Baron's' large fighter group as it swept overhead, spoiling for a fight. Later, they learned to keep their heads down, for fighter pilots of both sides became adept at trench-strafing — flying low over enemy troops, spraying them with machine-gun fire and small bombs.

Nor were all the bombs dropped in 1914-18 so small. The Royal Air Force (which was produced by merging the R.F.C. and R.N.A.S. on April 1, 1918) was dropping 1,650-lb 'block-busters' from its big Handley Pages in the autumn of 1918. This was far more than the complete loaded weight of the Sopwith Tabloids used for the first successful raids by British bombers, on October 8, 1914.

The Tabloids belonged to Cdr. Samson's R.N.A.S. Squadron, based at Antwerp. With the city about to fall to the Germans, Sqdn. Cdr. Spenser Grey and Flt. Lt. Marix decided to have one last crack at the nearest Zeppelin bases. Spenser Grey failed to locate the Cologne Zeppelin

First Chief of the Air Staff in 1918 and architect of the modern Royal Air Force was the late Lord Trenchard, whose portrait appears on this page. His belief in the value of strategic bombing was influenced by the period he spent as commander of the R.A.F's Independent Force, formed to carry out a non-stop air offensive on the German homeland. Heart of the Force was its squadrons of

Handley Page twin-engined night bombers, *upper pictures below*. Developed originally for the Royal Naval Air Service, each of these aircraft was powered by two 250-h.p. or 360-h.p. Rolls-Royce Eagle engines and could carry one 1,650-lb. bomb or an equivalent weight of smaller weapons. Folding wings facilitated storage on the ground.

sheds in heavy mist and bombed the railway station instead. Marix dived on the sheds at Düsseldorf, released his tiny 20-lb. bombs at point-blank range, and had the satisfaction of seeing one shed erupt in flames 500 ft high, showing that he had destroyed a fully-inflated Zeppelin inside. Although damaged by ground fire, the Tabloid staggered back to within 20 miles of Antwerp and its pilot finished the trip on a bicycle borrowed from a friendly peasant.

Impressed, no doubt, by such success, the Admiralty ordered from the Handley Page company 'a paralyser' of a bomber so that they could make really hard and sustained attacks on Germany. Long before this aircraft was ready for service, it was Britain which felt the weight of enemy attacks. First came the Zeppelins — mighty airships, built around a rigid aluminium girder framework, up to 643 ft. long and able to carry a heavy load of bombs at up to 60 m.p.h. Their fate was sealed when fast fighter-planes entered service, armed with machine-guns which fired incendiary bullets. In the end, of 62 military Zeppelins built, 19 were shot down, 11 wrecked by bad weather and another 11 destroyed by accident or bombing in their sheds.

Their place in attacks on Britain was taken by German heavy bombers, of which the most famous were the Gothas. When these machines made daylight raids on London in June-July 1917, without any apparent opposition, there was such a public outcry that the government decided to create the Royal Air Force, as a completely independent service, controlled by its own Air Ministry. It proved to be one of the wisest moves in the history of military aviation. Freed of the shackles of control by the Army and Navy, the R.A.F. adopted a policy of defence through attack that was to assist victory in the first World War and play a major part in achieving it in the second.

First Chief of Air Staff was Major-General Sir Hugh (later Lord) Trenchard, who stands out as the great architect of modern air power. He was a remarkable character, because he had been so badly wounded while serving as a Captain in the South African War that his superiors found him a nice easy job to keep him occupied until he retired. This did not fit in with Trenchard's ideas and when

Had the War continued a little longer, the twin-engined Handley Page 0/400s of the Independent Force would have been supplemented by four-engined V/1500s, *below*, able to bomb Berlin from bases in the United Kingdom. Each of these aircraft spanned 126 ft. and had a take-off weight of nearly 13½ tons. Four 375-h.p. Eagle engines gave a top speed of 90.5 m.p.h. with up to 7,500 lb. of bombs.
A total of 255 V/1500s were ordered, but with the end of the War only eight were completed. One of these made the first flight from Britain to India in December 1918, so pointing the way to a whole series of great long-distance flights.

Aircraft performance did not advance greatly during the 1914-18 War. The best fighters of 1918 were, in fact, slower than the experimental S.E.4, *top picture, right*, built at the Royal Aircraft Factory in 1914. Greatest progress had been made in aero-engine design. Availability of engines like the superb Rolls-Royce Eagle, *centre*, enabled pilots to plan seriously for long-distance flights, even across the Atlantic. John Porte of England had been preparing for a trans-Atlantic attempt when the War started in 1914, using the Curtiss twin-engined flying-boat *America* (*bottom*). Good as this machine might have been, the possibility of success would have been quite small.

he heard in 1912 that the newly-formed Royal Flying Corps was to have a Central Flying School, at which all pilots would be trained, he decided to apply for a post there.

He was told that it might be possible if he learned to fly by the end of the month. So he simply went down to Brooklands to see his old friend 'Tommy' Sopwith and was soon airborne in a rather tired old Farman biplane, in the capable hands of the chief instructor of the Sopwith School. With only 50 h.p. to push its mass of struts and wires through the air at the best of times, the aircraft could only just stagger along with Trenchard's tall figure perched behind the instructor. The latter was, therefore, rather glad when his pupil flew the necessary 'figures of eight' with reasonable success and qualified for his Certificate.

Trenchard's subsequent climb to the top was meteoric. Only two months after learning to fly, he became an instructor at the Central Flying School. Eleven months later he was Assistant Commandant. Eleven more months and, with most of the R.F.C. in France, he found himself with a row of almost empty sheds, a few men who were unfit for overseas service and some aircraft that were unfit for anything at all. He was given the job of creating a new air force out of what was left in England, from which a constant stream of replacements could be sent to France to keep the first-line squadrons up to strength. He did the best he could for three months and was then sent to

France himself to command No. 1 Wing of the R.F.C.

Just before the start of the 'Fokker Scourge', Trenchard took over command of the entire R.F.C. on active service. When the Scourge was finished, he had the task of building up yet another air force from what had survived the Fokkers. He did it so well that it was the R.F.C. which soon held the initiative, with its D.H.4 day bombers carrying the war into the enemy camp.

With such a background, he was an ideal man to create a great new unified air force, by making the R.F.C. and R.N.A.S. into the R.A.F.; but his heart was still with the squadrons in action on the other side of the Channel. So, when he found he could not get along with the Secretary of State for Air, he resigned and went back to France. With a nucleus of day bombers from the former R.F.C. and the Handley Page 'paralysers' of the R.N.A.S., he built the Independent Air Force.

The war ended before the Force could reach its peak, using huge four-engined Handley Pages able to bomb Berlin non-stop from England; but enough had been achieved to prove the war-winning capabilities of air power. The lesson was there for the whole world to study — that entire cities might be wiped out by air attack in any future war. De Lana's fear had become fact and over in America Orville Wright commented sadly, 'What a dream it was; what a nightmare it has become'.

NO SEAS TOO WIDE

It is often claimed that aviation would have advanced much more slowly but for the two World Wars; but is this really true?

The finest fighters at the time of the Armistice in 1918 were the German Fokker D. VII and British Sopwith Snipe, which flew at 116-121 m.p.h. with engines of 185 h.p. and 230 h.p. respectively. Back in 1914, the Royal Aircraft Factory had built a beautifully streamlined biplane known as the S.E.4 which had a top speed of 135 m.p.h. on only 160 h.p.

Furthermore, there were still many designers who preferred monoplanes to biplanes before the war. In Britain they suffered a setback when monoplanes were banned by the War Office after a number of accidents. The ban was lifted by the time the war started; but the demand for large numbers of aircraft, to keep the squadrons in France up to strength, made the government concentrate on the kind of designs that were already in production, and twenty years were to pass before the advantages of the monoplane were again recognised fully.

In engine design, there were certainly tremendous advances during the first World War. The Gnome rotary was still supreme in France and England when it started; but attempts to develop a much more powerful version by mounting two rows of seven cylinders one behind the other, to produce a 160 h.p. fourteen-cylinder engine, were not very successful.

Germany had already turned to the liquid-cooled six-cylinder in-line Mercedes engine, which was not only capable of development to much higher powers but made possible the more streamlined noses of fighters like the Albatros series. Britain and France had by no means neglected such engines. Water-cooled Hispanos gave excellent service in the S.E.5 and Spad fighters; but it was the entry of Rolls-Royce into the aero-engine field in 1915 that marked the turning-point in engine development. By the end of the war, the Rolls-Royce Eagle VIII, with two banks of six cylinders, arranged as a Vee, was not only giving 360 h.p. but was far more reliable than most of its lower-powered predecessors. Without it, many of the great flights

The three Curtiss flying-boats of the U.S. Navy which left Newfoundland on May 16, 1919, to attempt the first trans-Atlantic flight, via the Azores, were very different from the little *America* of 1914. Each was powered by four 400-h.p. Liberty engines, giving a total power nearly ten times as great as that of the pre-war machine. Yet, of the three, only NC-4, *top picture*, succeeded in reaching Lisbon, on May 29.

Meanwhile, back in Newfoundland, mechanics were busy assembling the Vickers Vimy, *bottom*, powered by two 360-h.p. Rolls-Royce Eagle engines, in which Capt. John Alcock and Lt. Arthur Whitten-Brown were to try to make a non-stop flight to the British Isles.

Overloaded with 865 gallons of fuel, the Vimy staggered off the ground at St. Johns, Newfoundland, at 4.15 p.m. on June 14, 1919, and headed out over the Atlantic. Fifteen hours and fifty-seven minutes later, it touched down and almost overturned in a bog in Ireland.

For their great achievement, Alcock and Brown received a *Daily Mail* prize of £10,000 and knighthoods from King George V. Sir John Alcock did not live long to enjoy the fruits of success, being killed in a Vickers Viking amphibian on December 18 in that same year. Today, passengers arriving at London Airport on trans-Atlantic airliners pass this statue of the two British airmen who blazed the trail for them to follow.

made immediately after the first World War would have been hazardous if not impossible.

After what their aircraft had achieved in wartime, many designers and manufacturers expected a boom in civil flying in 1919. They were disappointed, for several good reasons. Most important of these was that the public as a whole was still not ready to fly. Nothing had happened to change the pre-war view that flying was for supermen, and when it became known that a one-way trip by air from London to Paris was likely to cost £15.15 s. (equivalent to at least £75 today), it was clear that the supermen would also need to be rich.

The first essential was to prove to the man in the street that flying was safe; the second was to open up air routes between the major cities of the world. Nobody had any real experience of airline operation. The Germans had, admittedly, carried 19,100 passengers on regular services between Lake Constance and Berlin, and on other routes, in 1912-14, but the vehicles used had been Zeppelin airships. These lighter-than-air craft still had some admirers; but the future seemed to lie with heavier-than-air machines. The Americans had operated a twice-daily flying-boat service across the 20 miles of Tampa Bay, Florida, for four months in 1914; but only one passenger was carried on each flight and these activities of the St Petersburg-Tampa Airboat Line were, therefore, of mainly historical interest. The airlines of 1919 had to begin from scratch.

A hint of what airline travel might be like was given on February 8, 1919, when a Farman Goliath twin-engined bomber, converted for passenger carrying, flew from Toussus le Noble, Paris, to Kenley aerodrome near London. As commercial flying had still not been permitted to restart, after the war, the passengers were all military; but the standard of comfort provided was strictly civil, with seats in an enclosed cabin, lunch in the air and even a bottle of champagne.

While British and French airlines planned to make such flights daily routine, far more exciting events were taking place on the other side of the Atlantic.

To encourage aviation progress, in 1906 the *Daily Mail* newspaper had offered a series of prizes ranging from £250 for a successful model aircraft to £1,000 for the first airman to fly the English Channel and £10,000 for the first to fly between its two publishing centres, London and Manchester, within 24 hours. A rival editor, with less faith in flying, wrote sarcastically that he would give £10 *million* to anyone who could link the two cities by air. Yet all of these prizes had been claimed by 1910. On April 1, 1913, the *Daily Mail* had put up a further £10,000 for the first flight across the Atlantic — a distance of nearly 2,000 miles — at a time when nobody had managed to cover more than 630 miles on less hazardous overland routes.

No achievement in flying history demanded greater courage or navigational skill than the first solo flight across the Atlantic by Charles Lindbergh on May 20-21, 1927. In the Ryan monoplane *Spirit of St Louis*, he covered the 3,600 miles from New York to Paris non-stop in 33½ hrs. A fuel tank extended the full depth of the cabin in front of his seat, so that he could see forward only by periscope. He had no radio and the aircraft's single Wright Whirlwind engine developed only 220 h.p. A vast crowd welcomed Lindbergh when he landed at Croydon Airport, near London, *top left*, shortly afterwards. Later, he was often accompanied by his wife, Anne, *top right*.

First flight over the North Pole was made on May 9, 1926, by Lt. Cdr. (later Rear-Admiral) Richard Byrd, U.S.N., in the three-engined Fokker *Josephine Ford* (*lower picture*), piloted by Floyd Bennett. Three years later, Byrd was first to fly over the South Pole also, in a Ford Tri-motor piloted by Bernt Balchen, one of the greatest Arctic fliers of all time.

Airline services followed in the wake of the trailblazers. Pioneer companies like Aircraft Transport & Travel began with converted bombers like the D.H.9, *top left*, with the passengers either muffled in leather coats and helmets or packed inside primitive cabins. Standards improved quickly and by 1922 Daimler Airway offered first class service on board its D.H.34's. Steward Sanderson of Daimler, *top right*, was the first person employed by an airline to serve refreshments in flight. Another Daimler innovation, *centre left*, entailed fitting out the cabin of a D.H.34 to carry a spare engine for any of its aircraft stranded overseas by engine trouble.

First link in the chain of Imperial Airways' services throughout the British Empire was forged when the R.A.F's Cairo-Basra air mail route was taken over in 1926. Imperial's D.H.66 Hercules airliners were intended to fly on to Delhi, *bottom picture*, but the Persians refused at first to allow foreign aircraft to fly over their country and passengers had to transfer to ships at Basra.

Although it was 'April Fool's Day', nobody ridiculed the offer this time!

One man even began to plan how he would win the prize. Named John Porte, he was test pilot for the White and Thompson Company which held the British agency for flying-boats designed by Glenn Curtiss. He went over to the States and supervised the construction of a small twin-engined flying-boat, the *America*, in which to attempt an Atlantic crossing. Perhaps fortunately, war began before the aircraft was completed. Porte came back to England, closely followed by two Curtiss flying-boats based on the *America*. From these he evolved the larger 'boats used so successfully by the R.N.A.S. for anti-submarine and anti-Zeppelin patrols.

Curtiss, too, continued to build bigger and better flying-boats for the U.S. Navy, culminating in four large four-engined machines known as NC-1, 2, 3 and 4. Damaged in a hangar fire, NC-2 was dismantled and used as a source of spares for the other three which, on May 8, 1919, left Rockaway, Long Island, on the first leg of an attempted transatlantic flight. Nothing had been left to chance. No fewer than 27 naval destroyers were strung out along stage two of the route between Newfoundland and the Azores, each equipped with searchlights and signal rockets to assist the navigation of the flying-boat crews, and ready to provide an emergency rescue service. Five battleships, five cruisers and two tankers provided similar help between the Azores and Lisbon.

Despite all this, only one of the 'boats, NC-4, completed the crossing. NC-1 force-landed 200 miles short of the Azores and was abandoned. The pilot of NC-3 alighted on the sea at night in the hope that he would be able to fix his position more accurately in daylight. In doing so, the 'boat became so badly damaged that it was able to reach the Azores only by taxiing 200 miles through choppy seas.

The Atlantic had been crossed, but NC-4's achievement was completely outclassed on June 14-15, 1919, when Captain John Alcock and Lt. Arthur Whitten-Brown made a non-stop crossing from St John's, Newfoundland, to Clifden in Ireland in about 16 hours, compared with NC-4's 11 days from Newfoundland to Lisbon.

Today, when it is possible to cross the Atlantic in 6¼ hours in air-conditioned luxury on board a jet airliner, it is a sobering thought to go to the Science Museum and look at the comparatively small wood and canvas Vickers Vimy bomber flown by Alcock and Brown. It is easy to imagine what they endured in its open cockpit, cut off from the world soon after take-off when their radio packed up. The weather at times was so bad that the Vimy's wings became loaded with ice and they fell thousands of feet out of control, ending up almost on their back a few hundred feet above the stormy sea. Several times Brown had to

Anthony Fokker once described the Handley Page H.P.42 airliners of Imperial Airways as having built-in headwinds. With a cruising speed of only 100 m.p.h., they were certainly slower than many of their foreign competitors in the 1930s, but so great was the comfort they offered and so outstanding their safety record that they carried more passengers between London and the Continent than all other airliners combined. Only eight were built, of which four were 38-seaters based at Croydon, the others 24-seaters based in Cairo and used for services to Karachi and Cape Town. Behind the H.P. 42 *Helena* in the upper picture is the Croydon control tower.

Aircrew uniforms underwent big changes in the early 1930s. As the H.P.42 had an enclosed cockpit, its pilots exchanged leather coats, helmets and goggles for blue serge uniforms and peaked caps. An even greater change came on May 15, 1930, when Boeing Air Transport employed the first airline stewardesses, *bottom picture*, to serve passengers flying on its San Francisco-Chicago route; all were fully trained nurses.

clamber out on to the wing to hack away ice that was choking the Eagle engines. And even after they reached Ireland, fate dealt them one more cruel blow. What looked like a green meadow proved to be a bog in which the Vimy upended itself on to its nose as it landed.

Alcock and Brown not only received their £10,000, but were knighted for their achievement. Today, visitors arriving by air at London Airport, Heathrow, pass a statue of the two men, reminding them that their smooth flight was made possible only by the courage and skill of such pioneers.

The same combination of Vimy aircraft and Rolls-Royce Eagle engines made practicable the first flights from Britain to Australia and South Africa in 1919-20. In the years that followed, almost every major air route in the world was opened up by men of many nations. Some are remembered among the great names of history, like Charles Lindbergh, who made the first solo Atlantic flight in May 1927, and Sir Charles Kingsford Smith who, with a crew of three, made the first flight across the vast Pacific, from San Francisco to Brisbane, Australia, in a three-engined Fokker monoplane in 1928. Others like Floyd Bennett, who piloted Admiral Byrd on the first crossing of the North Pole, are almost forgotten, yet no less great.

In the slipstream of these pioneers came the airlines, gradually spreading their spider's web of services across the map. But although aviation was beginning to become

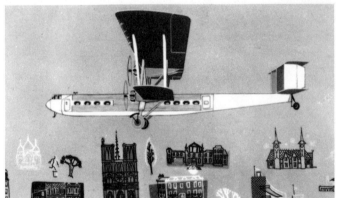

BETWEEN THE WARS The illustrations below and on the opposite page show four of the best-remembered aeroplanes of the 1920s and '30s. The Bristol Bulldog, *upper picture, this page*, was a standard R.A.F. single-seat fighter from 1929 to 1937, its biplane wings and 490-h.p. Bristol Jupiter radial engine being typical of its period. Carrying two machine-guns — an armament unchanged since the 1914-18 War — it had a top speed of 174 m.p.h. and took 14½ minutes to climb to 20,000 ft. Beneath the Bulldog is a photograph of a Ford Tri-motor transport, a type first produced in 1926. This particular example is still flying on local airline services in America. Even more remarkable is that a U.S. company is planning to put into production an updated version of the Ford, which was known usually as the 'Tin Goose'.

By the early 1930's the swing from biplane to monoplane was under way, particularly in America. The advantages were well demonstrated by the Boeing P-26A fighter, *upper picture*. Compared with its immediate predecessor, the Boeing P-12F biplane, the P-26A had an engine of the same power (600-h.p. Pratt & Whitney R-1340) but was 39 m.p.h. faster, with a top speed of 234 m.p.h. The example shown was still first-line equipment in Guatemala until 1955, when it was shipped back to America, overhauled and painted in the 1935-37 insignia of the 34th Pursuit Squadron, U.S.A.A.F.

Despite its biplane layout, the Fairey Swordfish torpedo-bomber, *lower picture*, was a later design than the P-26A and did not enter service with the Fleet Air Arm until 1936. Top speed was only 139 m.p.h., but the Swordfish — known affectionately as 'Stringbag' by its crews — was highly manoeuvrable and remained in service throughout World War II.

commercial and professional, it still felt like flying — and a personal adventure — even to the passengers. This was hardly surprising when we take a look at what it was like to fly on even a highly organised route like London to Paris when international services began on August 25, 1919.

First company to operate regularly between the British and French capitals was Aircraft Transport and Travel Ltd. Like the Farman company, it used converted bombers, but these were not big twin-engined machines, with lunch and champagne laid on for the customers. They were D.H.4 and D.H.9 single-engined day bombers, with two wicker seats crammed into the rear cockpit that had once housed the observer and his gun.

People who arrived at the grass aerodrome at Hounslow to travel in these aircraft discovered that, then as now, British airlines took good care of their passengers. Instead of expecting the ladies to clamber up the foot- and hand-holds in the side of the fuselage, A.T. & T. provided a sturdy household step-ladder. There was no air conditioning or heating, but each passenger was lent a long leather coat, helmet, goggles and gloves, plus a hot water bottle on really cold days.

There was no properly organised 'met' service and no radio on board the aircraft. Once off the ground, the pilot was on his own, although the Dutch airline K.L.M. did provide some kind of weather information for its pilots before they crossed the Channel coast *en route* for England. This involved circling round the back garden of a house belonging to one of the airline's employees, who chalked on a large blackboard whether or not the weather over the sea was sufficiently clear to fly through. If it was not, this presented little difficulty, as the airliners of 1919-20 were small enough and light enough to land in any decent-size field.

The only navigation aid available to pilots was a compass, which was not always reliable with so much metal near it. So it was usual to follow roads and railway lines. This led to an unfortunate mid-air collision one day when the pilot of a Paris-bound airliner had his head over the side of the cockpit, looking at the road below, at the same moment as the pilot of a London-bound airliner flying at the same height along the same road. But accidents were rare and the standard of service gradually improved.

Most enterprising of the early companies was the Daimler Airway, which introduced the first specially-designed airliners on its routes to Paris, Brussels, Amsterdam and Cologne. Its D.H.34's each carried nine passengers in wicker seats inside a roomy cabin, where they were served with tea and refreshments by the first air stewards employed anywhere in the world. There was a separate hold for baggage, and maintenance was studied as carefully as passengers' convenience.

Big problem, then as now, was to make airline services

pay. Competition from other companies and the reluctance of the public to fly, caused airline after airline to go out of business, and a sigh of relief went up in Britain when the handful of small struggling companies were united to form Imperial Airways, under government sponsorship, in 1924. This set the pattern for most countries, which either merged smaller companies into state-owned national airlines or encouraged private companies to grow by providing large subsidies for the carriage of air mail.

Throughout the 1920s and much of the '30s mail was more important than passengers. It provided a reliable, growing income throughout the whole year, and could be crammed on board without requiring any special furnishings or attention in flight. In fact, it was difficult to think of a more attractive payload. Thus, when Imperial Airways ordered a new fleet of three-engined D. H. Hercules aircraft in 1925, it asked for 465 cu. ft. of mail space and seats for only seven passengers. These aircraft were used on the first section of Imperial's proposed route to India. Surprisingly, this linked Cairo and Basra, across the desert; but the reason is simple to explain. Imperial simply took over an existing mail route that had been run by the R.A.F., at a time when it was impossible to fly all the way from London to the Middle East, as France would not allow the airline to fly across its territory.

International squabbles held up air travel in this way for years. After flying from London to Paris or Basle, passengers had to go by train to Brindisi where, eventually, they were able to catch a flying-boat for the overwater trip to Alexandria and then switch to a landplane for the rest of the journey to India.

Such a trip was planned carefully as a major expedition, and night stops were made at all kinds of exciting places. The landing sites in the desert, for example, were Foreign Legion-type forts in territory where the Arabs were by no means friendly. Having made such a journey, a passenger had plenty to talk about for months. This was *real* flying, at a speed and height which enabled passengers to see places of interest they passed over *en route* — very different from today's rocket-like flights above the clouds.

As airlines became financially more sound, they were able to afford better aeroplanes. Twin-engined, three-engined and even four-engined types became standard, to ensure safety in the event of an engine failure. Radio for communications and direction-finding came into use; so did 'met' services. In 1927, Imperial Airways offered passengers full-course hot meals for the first time on its *Silver Wing* lunchtime service to Paris. With the introduction of the big Handley Page H.P.42 in 1931, even the pilot was given an enclosed cabin for the first time, and was able to discard his leather coat, helmet and goggles in favour of a blue serge uniform, cap and gold braid.

Surprisingly, America was slow to follow Europe's lead

Two aircraft which speeded the transition from biplane to monoplane design were the Supermarine S.6 Schneider Trophy seaplane, *top*, and Douglas DC-1 airliner, *bottom*. The S.6 was not only one of the most streamlined aircraft of its day, but was also tremendously powerful, with a Rolls-Royce engine of 1,900 h.p. Piloted by Flying Officer H.R.D. Waghorn, it won the 1929 contest for the Schneider Trophy at an average speed of 328.63 m.p.h. Two years later, the improved S. 6B, with a 2,300-h.p. engine, won the Trophy outright for Britain and put the World Speed Record above 400 m.p.h.

From the S.6 and S.6B was evolved the famous Spitfire fighter of World War 2. From the DC-1 airliners was developed the DC-3 (Dakota), one of the greatest transport aeroplanes in history (see page 84).

in opening up airline services. The leadership given by the Wrights had soon been lost, and even when America entered the first World War in 1917, it could not organise its aircraft industry quickly enough to get a single combat aeroplane of U.S. design to France in time to play any part in the fighting.

Air mail services were operating across America by the early 1920s, but were flown by open-cockpit D.H.4's of British design. The only really important development was the setting up of strings of beacons to guide the mail pilots at night and in bad weather, and this marked the start of really efficient navigation aids for commercial flying. The only other U.S. innovation of any note in this period was the introduction of the first airline stewardesses — all trained nurses — by Boeing Air Transport in May 1930. They were not greeted very enthusiastically by pilots, who considered flying to be a man's game. But after these highly-trained young ladies had coped successfully with a number of emergencies, the pilots gradually changed their attitude.

The biggest revolution as the 1920s gave way to the 1930s was in the shape and performance of aircraft. For years after the first World War, air forces had had to make do with fighters and bombers left over from those used in action; but when replacements became essential the opportunity was taken to switch from wood to metal for their basic structure, although most were still covered with fabric.

FOUR KINDS OF FLYING From the simple aeroplanes of the early years have evolved many different forms of flying machine. The versatile Westland Wessex helicopter illustrated below seems remote from the theories of the early pioneers.

The Bloodhound anti-aircraft missile, *lower picture on this page*, may not look much like an aeroplane. In fact, that is what it is. It is steered in flight by movement of the pivoted wings. Four solid-propellent rockets accelerate it to the speed at which its ramjet engines can take over for cruising flight.

The Crusader naval fighter, *opposite, top*, is about to be catapulted from the deck of a large aircraft carrier. The speed imparted by the catapult, added to the forward speed of the ship, enables naval aircraft to take off after a very short forward run.

Fastest aeroplane yet flown, the North American X-15 rocket-powered research aircraft, *opposite, bottom*, is launched in mid-air, like a bomb, from beneath the wing of a Stratofortress 'mother-plane'. Before completing its flight test programme in 1968, it attained a speed of 4,534 m.p.h. and climbed to a height of 354,200 ft.

The promise of the monoplane was richly fulfilled in the aircraft illustrated on this page and opposite. Predecessor of the DC-1 (see page 81), the Boeing 247 of 1933, *top picture, this page*, was the first all-metal streamlined monoplane airliner built in America. Introducing refinements such as a retractable undercarriage, control surface trim-tabs, variable-pitch propellers, an automatic pilot and de-icing equipment, it reduced the U.S. transcontinental flight time to under 20 hours, carrying 10 passengers. Shown beneath it is a Douglas DC-3 (Dakota), of which more than 10,000 were built.

The two photographs opposite show some of the first Supermarine Spitfire fighters delivered to the R.A.F. Last great design by R.J. Mitchell, whose seaplanes had won the Schneider Trophy, the Spitfire and its partner, the Hawker Hurricane, were to turn the tide of war by winning the Battle of Britain in 1940. Both began as eight-gun monoplanes, with top speeds 100 m.p.h. faster than the biplanes they replaced.

An even more significant development was the gradual reappearance of the monoplane. Britain again pointed the way with its victories in the seaplane races for the coveted Schneider Trophy. The aircraft which beat all comers, and raised the world speed record above 400 m.p.h. for the first time in the process, were beautifully-streamlined metal monoplanes designed by R. J. Mitchell of the Supermarine company and powered by mighty 12-cylinder Rolls-Royce engines giving no less than 2,300 h.p.

Nobody could dispute the superiority of the monoplane any longer, and it was at this stage that America's aircraft industry began to show its capabilities. Monoplane airliners were not new. The Fokker company, in particular (formed in Holland after the war by Anthony Fokker) had specialised for years in highly-efficient three-engined monoplanes; but the Boeing 247 of 1933 was something quite different. It was a finely streamlined all-metal low-wing monoplane, powered by two 550-h.p. engines and with an undercarriage that retracted to reduce drag in flight. The pitch (or twist) of its propellers could be varied for maximum efficiency both during take-off and in cruising flight. The control surfaces were fitted with trim-tabs, enabling the pilot to 'balance' the aircraft so finely in flight that he could sit back and let an automatic pilot take over the donkey work of handling the controls.

First twin-engined monoplane able to climb on one engine with a full load, the 247 revolutionised air transport, cutting the U.S. transcontinental flight time to under 20 hours with 10 passengers. It was followed by the even better Douglas DC-1 and DC-2 and then the DC-3 Dakota, most famous airliner of all time and still in worldwide service more than 30 years after its first flight.

Military aircraft also switched to monoplane layout, as prototypes of aircraft that were later to become famous began to appear in growing numbers. Typical was the British Spitfire, a tiny but deadly little all-metal fighter, based by R.J. Mitchell on experience gained with his Schneider Trophy seaplanes. Armament increased from two to eight guns; cockpits became enclosed, undercarriages retracted and flaps were added to improve take-off performance and shorten landing runs.

Some biplanes remained, particularly for sport. Back in 1925, de Havilland had built a little two-seater named the Moth, which sold for only £595 and had folding wings so that it could be towed behind a car and kept in a garage. No toy, it was used by courageous men and women for almost unbelievable long-distance flights. Amy Johnson even flew one solo across half the world, from Britain to Australia. In such machines, it was still possible to fly like the birds, to feel the wind on one's face in an open cockpit, to loop, spin, feel carefree at little more cost than running a car. But time was running out for those who loved this kind of flying.

THE AIR WAR 1939-45

Within minutes of the declaration of war on September 3, 1939, air raid warning sirens sent Londoners scuttling for shelter. They had few illusions about what lay ahead. Many had considered war inevitable since the mid-1930s when the German dictator, Adolf Hitler, began the process of aggression and terrorisation that brought the Rhineland, the Saar, Austria and Czechoslovakia into his clutches.

The creation of the *Luftwaffe* (the German air force) had taken place secretly, in defiance of the 1919 Peace Treaty. When it was revealed in 1935, its size and the quality of its aircraft had come as a shock to France, Britain and other nations that had good reason to fear a rebirth of German militarism. Nor had minds become any easier when Germany and Italy, land of the other Fascist dictator Mussolini, despatched air forces to support General Franco during the Spanish Civil War. Memories of what German bombers had done to the almost defenceless town of Guernica were still fresh in September 1939 and it was easy to picture similar scenes of death and destruction in the great cities of Europe.

That first air raid alert was a false alarm, and so were some of the worst fears of the Londoners. They were to suffer grievously later, but Britain was not Spain and the Royal Air Force was not overawed by the numerical superiority of its enemy. In the Hurricane and the Spitfire, it had two of the finest fighter aircraft imaginable. On seeing the latter for the first time, the German Air Attaché to Britain had regarded its small size and beautiful lines with contempt, calling it a toy: his colleagues were soon to learn how very wrong he was. More important, the first radar aerials were going up around the British coast. By detecting and locating enemy aircraft while they were still many miles away, these invisible 'eyes' would avoid the need for defending fighters to maintain standing patrols, and so enable each squadron to do the work of two or three, without straining its pilots to breaking point.

Nor had Britain neglected its bomber force. The new Wellington and Hampden monoplanes were as efficient as they could be at a time before their pilots had electronic aids to help them locate their targets. And on the drawing boards and in the experimental workshops of Britain's aircraft industry, a new generation of four-engined bombers of unprecedented striking power — named Stirling, Halifax and Lancaster — was taking shape.

Most important of all was the heritage left by Trenchard, when he planned the future of the R.A.F. after the first World War. With the support of Winston Churchill, he had fought off all attempts by the older Services to have the air force split up once more into Army and Navy wings, under their control. This policy was changed slightly in 1937, after aircraft carriers had reached such a degree of importance and efficiency that carrier-based squadrons of the Fleet Air Arm were transferred to Admiralty control; but the land-based squadrons of Coastal Command remained part of the R.A.F., and the Air Ministry still had complete control of operations by Bomber Command, even when these were in direct support of the war on land or at sea.

Thus, on that September day in 1939, Britain had an air force that was not so large as that of its enemy, but was independent, equipped with aircraft second-to-none in quality and backed up by the electronic miracle of radar. But its greatest asset was the quality of its men.

In 1919, there had been no money for new aeroplanes. Having just won 'the war to end wars', the British government allocated so little cash to the Air Ministry that Trenchard had decided to spend most of it on training. His aim was to create a nucleus of highly-trained officers and men with what he called the 'air force spirit'. Better aeroplanes could come later. He was, he said, laying the foundations for a castle; if no-one built anything bigger than a cottage on them, it would at least be a very good cottage! Now, the cottage was under siege, and the scene from its windows was pretty frightening.

The *Luftwaffe* was still primarily a tactical air force, intended to support the operations of the German army, at the beck and call of army officers — and this appeared to work. Within little more than a month, Hitler's *blitzkrieg* (lightning war) tactics had added Poland to the territory of his Third Reich, which he boasted would last for a thousand years. Nothing, it seemed, could withstand the onslaught

Junkers Ju 87 dive-bombers blasted a path ahead of the German armies which subdued Poland in little more than a month in 1939 and went on to conquer Norway, Denmark, Holland, Belgium and France in a few weeks in 1940. This was the *blitzkrieg*, or 'lightning war', made possible by highly-mechanised forces. To add to the terror and confusion caused by their steeply-diving attacks, the Ju 87s often had screaming sirens mounted on them. Against weak defences such tactics could not fail and this obscured the fact that the Ju 87 was itself almost defenceless against determined fighter attack. When it was matched against the R.A.F. in the summer of 1940, even escorting fighters like the Messerschmitt Me 110 shown in the lower picture could not give it adequate protection and it played little part in the Battle of Britain.

Although R.A.F. Fighter Command had only 704 aircraft with which to meet the onslaught of 3,500 German combat machines at the start of the Battle of Britain, 620 were Hurricanes and Spitfires. Finest fighters in the world, they were flown by men who were unbeatable, serviced by seemingly tireless ground crews and supported by the miracle of radar which, by detecting every enemy attack, avoided the need for maintaining standing patrols of defending fighters. By the end of the Battle of Britain, the *Luftwaffe* had lost 1,733 aircraft and so many of its finest aircrew that it never recovered completely its old assurance and effectiveness. Cost to the R.A.F. was 915 aircraft, but many pilots parachuted to safety.

The pictures below show a Hurricane being re-armed, pilots relaxing briefly between 'scrambles' and Hurricanes on the warpath.

After the Battle of Britain had been won, the R.A.F. switched gradually to the attack. The support which it gave to the Allied armies as they drove back the enemy, first in North Africa and then in Europe, is symbolised in the upper picture on this page. It shows a Spitfire being serviced on an airfield in Sicily captured from the Germans. An abandoned Messerschmitt Bf 109 fighter stands forlornly in the background.

Realising that war with Hitler's Germany was almost inevitable, the R.A.F. had conceived a new generation of mighty four-engined bombers in 1936. First to enter service, in February 1941, was the Short Stirling, *lower picture*, which could carry seven tons of bombs for 590 miles and was armed with eight machine-guns.

of German armoured divisions backed up by the terrifying attacks of Junkers Ju 87 dive-bombers.

In the west, this was the period of the 'phoney war' — months in which the R.A.F. dropped propaganda leaflets instead of bombs on Germany, while the opposing armies viewed each other from the underground concrete forts of the Maginot and Siegfried Lines. Suddenly, in the spring of 1940, the *blitzkrieg* began again. Within weeks Norway, Denmark, Holland, Belgium, even the once-mighty France had fallen to Hitler's tanks and dive-bombers. The futility of concrete defences like the Maginot Line was proved for all time. The Germans did not even bother to attack this Line, they simply went round one end of it.

Hitler stated that he had now only to 'wring the chicken's neck' of Britain; to which Britain's new leader, Winston Churchill, replied: 'Some chicken, some neck' — and so it proved.

As a prelude to Operation Sealion, the invasion of England, the Germans had to destroy the Royal Air Force. This did not appear too difficult. They had been able to wipe out whole squadrons of the R.A.F.'s Battle bombers despatched on suicidal raids to destroy bridges in front of the German armies advancing in Western Europe. They had more respect for Fighter Command's Hurricanes and Spitfires, but there were so few of them.

There would have been even fewer if the Commander-in-Chief of Fighter Command, Air Chief Marshal Sir Hugh Dowding, had given in to French requests that the whole of his force should be flung into the battle on the other side of the Channel; but he knew this would make no difference to the outcome, and would only leave Britain defenceless afterwards. So, with Churchill's assent, most of the fighters stayed in Britain; although they did play a major rôle in enabling the British army to be taken off the beaches of Dunkirk, by keeping the *Luftwaffe* at bay further inland.

If war had come in 1938, as seemed likely at the time of the German take-over of part of Czechoslovakia, Fighter Command would have had only 93 Hurricanes and Spitfires, plus 573 outdated biplanes, to oppose about 1,200 modern German bombers. The year of grace, gained by the apparent weakness of Prime Minister Neville Chamberlain, enabled the force of modern eight-gun monoplane fighters to grow to 500 by the outbreak of war. Now, as Britain awaited Hitler's all-out attack in August 1940, Dowding had under his command 704 serviceable aircraft, of which 620 were Hurricanes and Spitfires. Opposing him were the 3,500 aircraft of Air Fleet 2 under Kesselring, Air Fleet 3 under Sperrle and Air Fleet 5 under Stumpff. Only now, looking back, can we see that the R.A.F. was superior to the *Luftwaffe* in everything but numbers.

The dive-bombers that had swept a path through Europe for Hitler's armies proved so vulnerable to determined attack by modern fighters that they achieved little. Mass

Attack from the air took a variety of forms as the war progressed. Germany opened the new age of 'push-button' warfare with its V-1 flying-bombs and V-2 long-range rockets, launched against London and other targets in 1944-45. No defence against the V-2, *top, right*, was possible, but the attack was halted when the Allies overran the launch-sites in Western Europe. At sea, carrier-based attack bombers like the Douglas Dauntless, *second picture from top*, turned the tide of the Pacific War, sinking four Japanese carriers at Midway alone. The next picture shows torpedo-bombers and fighters massed on the deck of a British carrier. Most incredible weapon of all was, perhaps, the Ohka rocket-powered suicide bomber, *bottom*, which Japanese *Kamikaze* pilots dived into Allied ships.

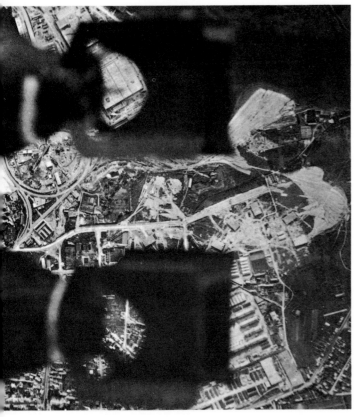

raids by hundreds of twin-engined bombers escorted by hundreds of fighters achieved more, because of the very weight of their attack, but they paid a terrible price. The harvest fields of Southern England soon bore a strange crop of wrecked aircraft marked with the black cross of Germany, and the *Luftwaffe* lost so many of its finest, most experienced crews that it never regained its old efficiency.

British and German statisticians disagree on the number of aircraft of each side that were lost in the Battle of Britain — as if it really mattered. The significant fact is that Britain, and the whole civilised world, had been saved by the quality of 704 aeroplanes and the courage and self-sacrifice of 1,000 pilots of the R.A.F. who refused to be beaten.

The war was to continue for five more grim years, and was to extend over almost the whole world, bringing in countries like America, Japan and Russia; but after the Battle of Britain, defeat for the Allied cause was unthinkable.

Driven from the daylight skies, the *Luftwaffe* turned to night bombing, and London's ordeal began in earnest. Then the R.A.F. began to hunt down the enemy bombers at night with the aid of radar carried in its fighters. Soon, even the darkness no longer provided cover for the twin-engined Heinkels, Dorniers and Ju 88s, and the night bombing ceased. Hit-and-run daylight raids by fighter-bombers were to continue throughout the war, supplemented in 1944-45 by the Wellsian offensive of Germany's V-wea-

pons — the V-1 flying-bomb and V-2 rocket. But, although brilliantly conceived, these first robot missiles were an admission of defeat. They had to be used because the piloted aircraft of the *Luftwaffe* had been beaten. Their offensive failed because it was already too late — the launch-sites were quickly destroyed or captured, and the factories producing them were bombed so heavily that the attack was only a fraction of the overwhelming war-winning onslaught that Hitler had planned. Furthermore, Fighter Command's equipment had become so fine that its pilots were able to shoot down the V-1s with almost contemptuous ease.

Instead of England, it was Germany which learned the true terror of modern air attack. Under a non-stop offensive, by R.A.F. Bomber Command at night and the U.S. Army Air Forces by day, its cities crumbled and burned, its factories were obliterated, the oil essential to keep its armies on the move ceased to flow. Two million Germans spent their time on anti-aircraft duties, trying to repel the air armadas and repair the ravages when the bombers had gone. They were too few to prevent the destruction of 500 acres or more in the heart of 31 cities and the death of 305,000 of their people. A further 7½ million were rendered homeless. Having sown the wind, Germany reaped the whirlwind.

Even at sea, the aircraft carrier replaced the battleship as the spearhead of a navy's fighting strength. The deadly

Famous aircraft and famous ship. The picture on the opposite page shows a Swordfish torpedo-bomber circling over H.M.S. *Ark Royal*, most publicised Royal Navy carrier of World War II. The pilot of the Swordfish, Mike Lithgow, was also destined to become famous as a post-war test pilot and, for a time, holder of the world air speed record.

The aircraft which brought the war to an end was the Boeing B-29 Superfortress bomber, *below*. From island bases in the Pacific, it kept up a non-stop attack on the Japanese homeland from November 1944, dropping a total of 171,060 tons of high-explosive and incendiary bombs, plus 12,035 mines in Japanese waters. So ineffective were the enemy fighter defences against B-29s, which were able to fly at up to 30,000 ft., that all but the tail guns were removed from the bombers to save weight and so increase the bomb-load. The final blow fell on August 9, 1945, when the second atomic bomb, *lower picture*, was dropped on Nagasaki. Known as 'Fat Man', it was 10 ft. 8 in. long, 5 ft. in diameter, weighed about 4½ tons and had a destructive power equivalent to 20,000 tons of high-explosive. Six days later Japan surrendered.

As the war progressed, aircraft were modified to take on many jobs for which they had not been designed. Wellington bombers were fitted with 48-ft.-diameter metal hoops early in 1940 to explode German magnetic mines at sea. Havoc night fighters carried searchlights in their nose to illuminate enemy bombers for other fighter pilots to attack. Hurricanes, *below*, were fitted with 40-mm. guns, as big as light anti-aircraft guns, to attack and destroy German tanks in North Africa.

The end of the war did not bring the hoped-for era of peace and goodwill among the ex-Allies. In 1948-49, the Russian blockade of West Berlin brought the world to the brink of another great war, but the Berlin Air Lift proved that air power could prevent as well as win wars. In fifteen months, the American, British and French air forces, with the help of British civil charter firms, flew in 2,326,205 tons of supplies, *right*, to keep West Berlin alive and at work, until the blockade was lifted.

Battle of the Atlantic, which might have starved Britain into submission, was saved when aircraft from escort carriers, and long-range flying-boats and bombers from shore bases, were able to strike back at German submarines.

In the Pacific, the tide of Japanese success was turned in a succession of great sea battles, fought by naval aircraft without the crews of the opposing ships ever seeing each other. At Midway alone, American Dauntless dive-bombers sank four Japanese carriers. Each victory carried the Allied forces nearer to Japan; but final invasion of the enemy homeland was not necessary, as it had been in Europe.

American long-range bombers, operating from island bases recaptured from the Japanese, wrought wholesale destruction on enemy cities. The Japanese tried to hold back the Allied forces by the most desperate means, devising even special suicide aircraft in which pilots were able to win an honourable soldier's death by diving into British and American ships, blowing themselves to pieces with their enemies. All to no avail. Even before American Superfortresses dropped atomic bombs on Hiroshima and Nagasaki in August 1945, the war was virtually over. A single raid on Tokyo with incendiary bombs on March 9, 1945 had killed more people than either of the atomic weapons — and Japan had had enough.

By the time World War 2 was over, everyone had seen enough of war—or so it seemed. The aeroplane had done its job only too well. The last vestiges of the old 'knights in shining armour' kind of single-handed combat went with the end of the Battle of Britain. After that, air power became a relentless steam-roller against which nothing could survive, controlled by men but no longer bearing any resemblance to the kind of flying that had once seemed worth striving for.

The aeroplane had met every demand made upon it. When bombers had sought the cover of darkness, fighters had acquired radar to track them down and destroy them. When it was discovered in 1941 that Bomber Command was missing most of its targets, radio and radar aids were introduced which turned darkness into light. When there were tanks to be destroyed, fighters carried guns as big as anti-aircraft weapons, and rockets. When there were German dams to be breached, Lancaster bombers carried ingenious skipping weapons to do the job. When the Germans laid magnetic mines to sink British ships, Wellington bombers flew with great rings around them, to explode the mines harmlessly as they flew overhead. Yet all of these weapons and aids to destruction paled into insignificance by comparison with the atomic bomb. Having become the supreme instrument of destruction it seemed that the aeroplane might also have become so all-powerful that a third world war was already completely out of the question, for ever.

THE GREAT DETERRENT

Few people were naive enough to believe that the unconditional surrender of Germany and Japan, in 1945, had automatically solved all the problems of the world. In one respect, the world was more divided than ever, with the Western Allies in one camp and Russia, its sympathisers and satellites in the other. Most of the shooting had stopped, but the tension between East and West was so great that journalists and politicians began referring to it as the 'cold war'.

Periodically in the past 25 years there has arisen the possibility that the cold war might become hot. Almost always, air power, or the threatened use of air power, has persuaded one side to relent. We live in the age of the deterrent, of peace through fear. The cynic will say that it is better to be afraid than dead. Certainly, without the deterrent power of the atomic bomb and its even deadlier offspring, the hydrogen bomb, World War 3 would have begun long ago.

Human nature being what it is, nations have tried repeatedly to make gains at the expense of their neighbours without going far enough to risk an all-out nuclear war. The first occasion was in the summer of 1948 when, in an effort to get her former allies out of West Berlin, Russia imposed a blockade to prevent food and supplies from reaching the 2¼ million people in the Western half of the city.

At once the American, British and French air forces began flying food, equipment and supplies into West Berlin. Nobody thought that such an operation could be kept up for long, or could keep so many people adequately fed and at work. However, instead of collapsing, the great Air Lift grew week by week. The Dakotas used at first were replaced by larger American Skymasters and R.A.F. Yorks. Soon, the skies that a few years earlier had throbbed with the sound of bombers on their way to destroy a city, were filled with a great stream of transport aircraft, only two to five minutes' flying time apart, trying to keep that same city alive. Even bulk goods like coal, flour and petrol, which no-one would dream of carrying by air in normal circumstances, were flown into Berlin by the ton.

Next test of the Western Powers' willingness to resist aggression was the Korean War, which brought U.S. Superfortresses, *top picture*, into action once again. Most significant development in air power was, however, the emergence of the helicopter as a front-line vehicle to supply and support armies in the field.

The man who made the modern helicopter possible was a Spaniard, Juan de la Cierva. By inventing the 'flapping hinge' and fitting it to his fourth Autogiro, *lower picture*, which flew in January 1923,

he overcame the problem of unequal lift from the advancing and retreating blades which had caused earlier rotating-wing aircraft to overturn during take-off.

Greatest of the pioneers who took over from Cierva was Igor Sikorsky, who began building helicopters in Russia as early as 1909. When his second helicopter, *opposite*, *top*, failed to fly in 1910, he turned to fixed-wing aircraft and flew the world's first four-engined aeroplane, *opposite*, *bottom*, in May 1913.

From his first four-engined aeroplane, which he named *Le Grand*, Sikorsky evolved the improved *Ilia Mourometz* (*upper picture*). Among its unusual features were a ski undercarriage, for operation from snow, and a promenade deck above the fuselage on which passengers could walk in flight. More than 70 giant aircraft of this type flew with the Czar's Squadron of Flying Ships in the 1914-18 War. After the revolution, Igor Sikorsky went to America and started again. With little money, he designed the S-29A (A for America) and built it outdoors on a farm, *lower picture*. Parts came from scrapyards and when all his cash was spent he locked potential shareholders in a room until they produced sufficient money to complete the S-29A. When the aircraft was ready for its first flight, several of his loyal employees climbed on board. Too kindhearted to turn them off, Sikorsky nearly met with disaster when the overloaded and underpowered aircraft lost height and crashed. Undaunted, he rebuilt it and the subsequent success of the S-29A helped to put the young company on its feet.

For many years, Sikorsky was best-known for the amphibian airliners which he built for great companies like Pan American Airways. But he never lost his early interest in rotating-wing aircraft and on September 14, 1939, he flew the world's first entirely practical helicopter, the VS.300, *top*. Today, his is the most respected name in helicopter engineering.

Another tremendously important first flight had taken place secretly in Germany less than one month earlier, on August 27, 1939, when the Heinkel He 178 jet-plane, *centre*, took off for the first time. Britain was not far behind. Sir Frank Whittle had been first to run a jet-engine successfully on April 12, 1937, and was already working on improved versions, *bottom*, to power the earliest British jet aircraft.

As in wartime, the men seemed less significant than the machines they flew, the machines less important than what they carried. Only occasional reports of individual deeds of courage and skill reminded us that this was still flying, of a kind.

One such story followed the addition of commercial aircraft to the Air Lift armada, to carry special cargoes such as petrol. Chief tanker pilot was Air Vice-Marshal D.C.T. Bennett, wartime head of the R.A.F. Pathfinder Force which guided the bombers to their targets. After take-off one day, he suddenly realised with horror that someone had forgotten to remove the control locks which prevented the elevators of his aircraft from being blown up and down by the wind while parked on the ground. By using the remaining controls and trim-tabs, he succeeded in making a smooth circuit and a safe landing. Other pilots, confronted with other emergencies, were less lucky and a total of 51 Allied airmen died in 17 serious accidents during an operation that should never have been necessary.

At last, in May 1949, the Russians admitted they were beaten, and lifted the blockade. War had been averted for the first time by unarmed aircraft, for if the Air Lift had not succeeded the only alternative would have been to force a way through on the ground.

Subsequent wars, in Korea, Vietnam and elsewhere, have been more like the old-fashioned hot variety, but have stopped short of provoking the use of nuclear weapons. To cope with them, air forces have had to be prepared to fight any one of several widely-differing types of campaign at a moment's notice, using different weapons for each. Their ability to do so results from the fact that World War 2 produced three major new developments in air power, apart from the atomic bomb. The first was a new kind of aircraft — the helicopter; the second was a new power plant for existing aircraft — the jet-engine; the third was a new type of weapon — the guided missile.

As we have seen earlier, helicopters were making brief hops as early as 1907, but nobody produced a really practical rotating-wing aircraft until Juan de la Cierva of Spain perfected the Autogiro in 1923. This was only half-way-to a helicopter, as it could not make true vertical take-offs and landings, or hover: but it could take off and land much more slowly and in a much shorter distance than any aeroplane and, for this reason, offered a big improvement in safety. Ironically, Cierva himself was killed in 1936 when the airliner in which he was travelling crashed after take-off in fog — just the kind of accident that his slow-flying Autogiro had been designed to eliminate.

Key to both the success and limitations of the Autogiro was that its rotating wing, or rotor, was not driven by the engine but was simply turned automatically by the airflow passing by it, like the sails of a windmill. First to fly a completely practical helicopter, with powered rotor, was

AIR POWER IN THE 1960s The technique of refuelling one aeroplane from another in flight was tried out experimentally by pilots of the U.S. Army Air Service, flying D.H.4 day bombers, in 1923. It was perfected by Sir Alan Cobham's Flight Refuelling company in Britain and is today in everyday use as a means of extending the range and endurance of military aircraft. His 'probe and drogue' method is shown in use in the picture below, which depicts an F9F-8P Cougar reconnaissance-fighter of the U.S. Navy being refuelled by a KC-130F Hercules tanker of the Marine Corps.

One of the finest interceptor fighters in the world is the twin-jet BAC Lightning, *top right*, which is able to fly at more than twice the speed of sound and is armed with Firestreak or Red Top air-to-air missiles. These missiles home automatically on the hot exhaust from the engines of the enemy aircraft against which they are fired. The Lightning illustrated, from No. 111 Squadron, has streamed its tail parachute to slow it after landing.

For many years, the R.A.F. strike force was equipped with squadrons of Handley Page Victor, *bottom right*, and Hawker Siddeley Vulcan four-jet bombers, each carrying a Blue Steel air-to-surface rocket-powered missile with an H-bomb warhead. Today, Victors still serve for long-range reconnaissance and as flight refuelling tankers.

First British jet-plane to fly, on May 15, 1941, was the little Gloster E. 28/39 research aircraft. Top speed was about 300 m.p.h. with the original Whittle W. 1 turbojet engine of only 860 lb. thrust (equivalent to 688 h.p. at that speed). Thus, it flew nearly as fast as some of the first-line piston-engined fighters of its day on only half their power. When re-engined with a more powerful turbojet, it achieved 466 m.p.h. and climbed to a height of 42,000 ft. This offered great promise for the jet-fighters that were already taking shape in the Gloster factory.

Igor Sikorsky, on September 14, 1939. He had built his first helicopters back in 1909-10 in Russia; but realised that such aircraft were not practical at a time when so much remained to be learned about aerodynamics and lightweight structures and turned instead to aeroplane design. Within three years he had produced the world's first four-engined aeroplane, followed by an improved model complete with a cabin in which meals were served, a toilet and an open promenade deck above the fuselage on which any passenger who was sufficiently brave could walk during flight. Seventy more of these giant aircraft were built as bombers during the first World War, to equip the Czar's Squadron of Flying Ships, and made 400 successful raids for the loss of only one of their number.

Sikorsky left Russia for America after the Revolution and had to overcome tremendous problems before he was at last recognised as one of the world's greatest aircraft designers. Today his name is almost synonymous with the helicopter.

His counterpart in the jet-engine field is Sir Frank Whittle, who had to overcome equally frustrating setbacks before he could translate his theories into practical 'ironmongery'. He had realised as early as 1928, when he was a young cadet at the R.A.F. College, Cranwell, that aeroplanes would one day reach their limit in terms of speed and altitude unless some way could be found of replacing their pro-

pellers and piston-engines by a power plant that would operate efficiently in the 'thin' air above 30,000 feet.

Whittle was not the first to suggest that the solution lay in a jet-engine; but he was the first with sufficient determination and ability to face up to the problems of finding metals able to withstand the heat and stresses built up inside a jet-engine, and to overcome official disinterest. His efforts were rewarded on April 12, 1937 when his prototype engine ran successfully for the first time.

Although he could not know it then, another young designer, named Pabst von Ohain, was also working on jet-engines in Germany. Von Ohain's engine did not run as early as Whittle's but was the first to power an aeroplane in flight when the Heinkel He 178 experimental monoplane made the first-ever flight by a jet-plane on August 27, 1939.

The Gloster-Whittle E. 28/39, powered by an improved version of Whittle's engine, did not fly until May 15, 1941, but by then Gloster already had in production a twin-jet fighter named the Meteor to take advantage of this highly promising new form of propulsion. It has always been stated that the first jet-fighter to go into action in World War 2 was the German Messerschmitt Me 262; but the closest possible study of all available records appears to show that the honour really belongs to the Meteor, which became operational with No. 616 Squadron of R.A.F. Fighter Command in time to fly its first sortie against

First Squadron in the world to go into action with jet-fighters was No. 616 of the R.A.F., *top*, whose Meteors joined in the battle against Germany's flying bombs on July 27, 1944, and served subsequently in France. After the war, the Meteor further proved its capabilities by raising the world air speed record first to 606.38 m.p.h. and then to 615.81 m.p.h. At the time it did so, many experts believed that aeroplanes were approaching their limit in terms of speed because of the so-called 'sound barrier' that had already broken up many high-speed aeroplanes. The British government refused to allow British test pilots to try to break through the 'barrier', even though the Miles company had been building a special aircraft for the purpose. So, the first person to prove that a properly-designed aeroplane could fly faster than the speed of sound was Captain Charles Yeager of the U.S.A.F., in the Bell X-1 rocket-powered research aircraft, *bottom*. The X-1 was launched in mid-air from a B-29 mother-plane, *centre*.

SWEPT, STRAIGHT OR SWING WING? Most high-speed aeroplanes built since the war have had sweptback wings, like the Hawker Hunter fighters of the R.A.F's famous 'Black Arrows' aerobatic team, *top picture*. Sweepback postpones and minimises the effects of the shock-waves of air that build up when an aircraft approaches the speed of sound. However, the Bell X-1 proved that sweepback is not essential if an aircraft is built strongly enough and some supersonic aircraft, like the F-104 Starfighter, *lower picture*, have stubby straight wings.

In general, it can be said that straight wings are best at slower speeds, especially during take-off and landing, while sweptback wings are better at high speeds. "Swing-wing" aeroplanes, like the F-111 fighter-bomber, *opposite*, get the best of both worlds. During take-off and landing, their wings are only slightly swept. For high-speed cruising, the wings pivot back, as shown, giving almost a delta-wing shape as the wings and tailplane come together.

Largest rocket weapon in service in the world, this 114-ft. long Russian SS-9, intercontinental ballistic missile, *top left*, is known to NATO forces by the code-name 'Scarp'. It can lob a 25-megaton H-bomb warhead thousands of miles, or can orbit a warhead designed to attack American positions. Some experts still believe that manned bombers like Britain's missile-armed Vulcan, *top right*, are better than rockets. They can attack from high or low level, from any direction, can be switched to a different target or recalled in flight and can be 'scrambled' in under two minutes from their war stations.

America intended the XB-70A, *bottom*, to be its next long-range bomber, to supersede the Stratofortresses that are now in service. A change of policy led to cancellation of the project in favour of long-range missiles, but two XB-70As were completed for use as research aircraft. Their ability to cruise for long periods at three times the speed of sound (2,000 m.p.h.) at 70,000 ft. has provided data to speed America's supersonic airliner programme.

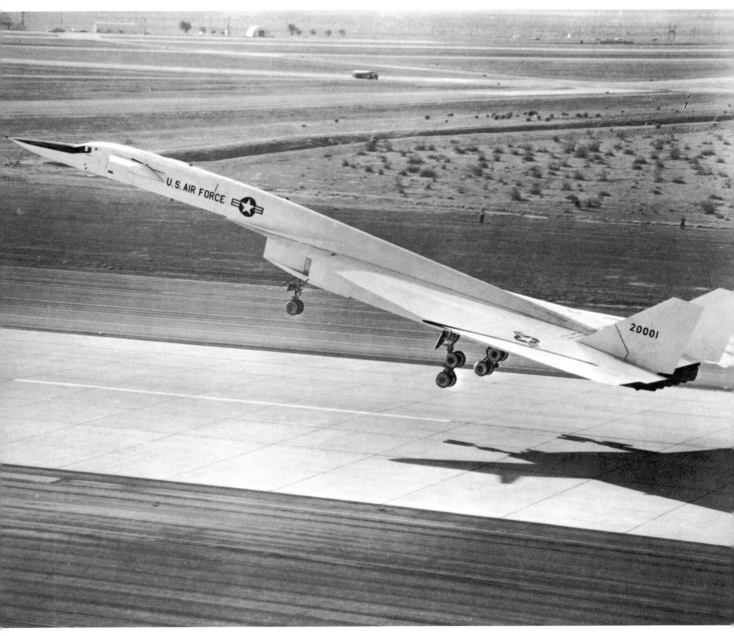

Mainstay of the U.S. Navy, U.S.A.F., R.A.F. and the fighter forces of other countries, the Phantom II, *top left*, is a two-seater which can carry a heavy load of air-to-air or ground attack weapons at 2 ½ times the speed of sound in all weathers. The Russian MiG-21, *top right*, is smaller, lighter and more limited in range, very easy to fly and has been exported to many of Russia's friends and allies; it is being built under licence in India. Another comparatively short-range, lightweight fighter is Sweden's J 35 Draken, seen inside camouflaged hangars at a dispersal station in the lower photograph. All three of these aircraft types can fly at twice the speed of sound and carry air-to-air missile armament.

German V-1 flying-bombs on July 27, 1944. The first Me 262s entered service with the K.G. 51 fighter-bomber group of the *Luftwaffe* in the following month.

From that moment, it was clearly only a matter of time before jet-planes replaced piston-engined fighters and bombers in all first-line combat units of the major air forces; but there was still one obstacle to higher performance that had to be overcome.

Pilots first encountered it when diving the fastest wartime piston-engined fighters at top speed. For no apparent reason, the aircraft suddenly began to judder violently, as if they were being hit by a huge sledge-hammer. Sometimes the buffeting became so bad that it ripped off the fighters' wings or tail and many lives were lost. Aerodynamicists knew the cause and called it 'compressibility'. They explained that as airflow over the wings of a high-speed aeroplane approached the speed of sound (760 m.p.h. at sea level, dropping to 660 m.p.h. above 36,000 ft.), shock-waves were created which caused the buffeting. By making wings thinner and by sweeping them backward, higher speeds could be attained before running into trouble; but nobody knew how to break through the 'sound barrier' to supersonic (faster-than-sound) speeds, or even if it was possible to do so.

The U.S. Air Force decided to find the answers and ordered from the Bell company a small, strongly-built rocket-powered research aircraft known as the X-1. To save fuel, this aircraft was carried to a height of 30,000 ft. under a converted Superfortress bomber and then dropped like a bomb. Its pilot was a young Air Force Captain named Charles 'Chuck' Yeager and he faced a frightening task. On each successive flight he got a little nearer to the speed of sound and by October 14, 1947 had come to within 6% of it, at the cost of a ride so rough that any other aeroplane would have disintegrated.

On that 14th day of October, he was determined to go all out in an attempt to smash through the 'barrier'. Opening up to full throttle after release from the Superfort, he felt the buffeting begin and the aircraft no longer seemed completely stable, but there was no turning back and his instruments showed that he must be nearly at the speed of sound. Suddenly, instead of getting worse, the hammering stopped. Yeager had become the first man in the world to prove that the speed of sound was really no barrier to a carefully-designed aircraft and that at supersonic speed all the unpleasant buffetings disappear. There was no longer any limit to aircraft speed and today it is quite normal for fighters to fly at up to 2¼ times the speed of sound (1,650 m.p.h.). Aircraft built of heat-resisting metals like stainless steel and titanium can fly even faster, and the North American X-15 rocket plane has clocked 4,534 m.p.h.—more than six and a half times the speed of sound.

Third of the great wartime developments—the guided

Most defence systems make use of both fighter aircraft and missiles nowadays. Fighters like the French Navy's Etendard, *left*, can often be operated as both interceptors and fighter-bombers. Alternative weapons carried by the Etendard include pairs of air-to-surface or air-to-air missiles, honeycomb packs of unguided rockets, bombs and 30-mm. guns. By comparison, surface-to-air missiles like the British Bloodhound, *right*, are single-shot weapons; but their speed, accuracy and ability to reach great heights very rapidly makes them ideal for dealing with enemy aircraft that have eluded the fighter screen. Bloodhound works in conjunction with powerful radars which detect the enemy aircraft and 'illuminate' it with their signals. As the radar signals bounce back from the bomber, Bloodhound picks them up and homes on to the point from which they are being reflected (i.e. the bomber). It is so effective that it was chosen by countries like Sweden and Switzerland against strong foreign competition.

missile—did not advance far by 1945. The German V-1 flying-bomb and V-2 rocket had only rudimentary guidance systems, but they pointed the way that has led to the whole vast array of modern guided missiles—ranging from air-to-air weapons used by fighters, which home on to the hot exhaust of enemy aircraft, to great intercontinental ballistic missiles, housed in bomb-proof underground launch-pits and armed with an H-bomb warhead.

To meet all its commitments, therefore, the modern air force requires a fantastic variety of weapons. A few high-speed long-range jet-bombers are retained by the major powers for use in an all-out nuclear war, carrying H-bomb air-to-surface rocket-powered missiles and electronic countermeasures equipment to jam enemy warning and anti-aircraft radar systems: but the main offensive strength of the U.S.A. and Russia consists of long-range missiles, housed both underground and at sea in hard-to-find submarines.

High-speed jet interceptor fighters, armed with homing missiles, are still in service to deal with enemy bombers; but these, too, have been replaced to a certain extent by surface-to-air missiles.

The most important elements of an air force are its squadrons of tactical fighters and bombers, as these are the aircraft best able to cope with the limited wars which are far more likely than an all-out nuclear slogging match.

They had their beginnings in the Allied tactical air forces of World War 2 and are sometimes organised as self-contained air forces in miniature. The R.A.F.'s No. 38 Group provides a good example as it has four-engined transports to fly assault troops quickly to a trouble spot, complete with their vehicles, guns and equipment, helicopters to keep up a shuttle service of supplies and to evacuate casualties, and jet fighter-bombers to provide air cover for the entire force.

Helicopters first came into their own in the Korean War, proving their ability to put down troops and equipment in almost inaccessible areas, under the very noses of the enemy, and to rescue the crews of aircraft shot down over land or sea. The death rate for wounded was cut to the lowest percentage in military history by flying them from front-line to hospital by helicopter. In fact, in military and civil use, the 'chopper' has become one of the most effective means of saving lives that has ever been devised; but it is not always so friendly. In Vietnam, U.S. helicopters have done deadly work with machine-guns, rockets and grenades in support of the ground forces to which they give mobility, while at sea helicopters can hunt and kill submarines with unrivalled efficiency. Their big advantages are that they can operate from small platforms on any kind of ship and hover while 'listening' for submerged submarines with sonar equipment, which is lowered into

Fighters and bombers are only two of the classes of aircraft needed by a major air force. Transport aeroplanes like the Lockheed C-130 Hercules, *left*, are essential, to move troops, equipment and supplies quickly to wherever they are needed. Such aircraft must be able to land on rough airstrips in combat areas. Helicopters, developed for transport duties, have many other uses. In peacetime, their ability to carry out search and rescue missions saves many civilian lives. Crewmen trained to be lowered by winch to snatch ditched airmen from the sea, or injured pilots from behind enemy lines, use their skill to save swimmers in difficulty and to haul sailors from wrecked ships. The dramatic photograph at the bottom of this page shows an airman of the R.A.F. Coastal Command going down from a hovering Whirlwind helicopter to rescue survivors from the French trawler *Jeanne Gougy*, wrecked off Land's End. *Top right*, an Iroquois armed helicopter of the U.S. army in a more aggressive mood, firing its rockets against ground targets.

The American parachute troops shown in the lower illustration on this page are demonstrating one of the earliest techniques used for almost vertical landing of soldiers and supplies in places far from aerodromes. The stone age people of New Guinea, *top left*, are quite familiar with the Bell Iroquois helicopters of the Royal Australian Air Force, although they have never seen a motor car, a railway train or a ship. Nor is there much limit to what helicopters can carry. Russia's giant Mil Mi-10 flying crane, *top right*, can lift lorries, guided missiles, even prefabricated buildings weighing up to 15 tons.

A completely new method of vertical take-off and landing, known as jet-lift, was pioneered in 1954, by Rolls-Royce's ungainly 'Flying Bedstead', *opposite page*. This contraption was thrust off the ground by directing vertically downward the exhaust of two jet-engines. To keep it balanced in flight, the pilot's controls ejected varying amounts of compressed air through downward-pointing nozzles at the front, back and on each side.

The jet-lift technique pioneered by the 'Flying Bedstead' has made possible the world's first vertical take-off combat aircraft, the R.A.F.'s Hawker Siddeley Harrier. In this case, the exhaust from a single jet-engine is directed downward by two pairs of rotating nozzles. When the Harrier has reached a safe height, its pilot gradually rotates the nozzles rearward. This causes the aircraft to accelerate until, after a time, the wings can provide all the lift needed for cruising flight. The nozzles are then rotated completely rearward, so that all the engine's thrust can be used for propulsion. The Harrier can hover and fly forward, backward or sideways. It is supersonic in a dive and can operate from anywhere that a helicopter can land. It carries its weapons under the wings and fuselage.

the water suspended from the end of a special cable.

The combination of anti-submarine helicopters, land-based tactical air forces and long-range strategic missiles has just about 'sunk' the aircraft carrier. Only America, with its immense resources, seems to consider the carrier worth keeping as a wide-ranging mobile airfield, capable of launching supersonic attack bombers, fighters to protect itself and other naval vessels, and anti-submarine aircraft. But the Royal Navy will continue to use smaller assault carriers as bases for troop-carrying helicopters.

Key to air power in this nuclear age is the ability to operate even in places where there are no proper airfields. Fighters and bombers have to be able to take off from short grass strips, and the ideal is a VTOL (vertical take-off and landing) aircraft able to operate from spaces as small as a jungle clearing, a strip of beach, a main road or a factory yard. One such aircraft is, of course, the helicopter; but it is not fast enough for some duties and the aircraft industries of the world have built aircraft with all kinds of weird shapes in an effort to combine the go-anywhere capability of the helicopter with the speed of a fixed-wing aircraft.

Britain has led the world in this exciting new kind of aviation. It all started back in 1954, when Rolls-Royce produced a machine so unlike any other aircraft that it was usually known as the 'Flying Bedstead'. The principle was simple enough. If a jet-engine developing, say, 5,000 lb. of thrust is mounted vertically in an aircraft, so that the exhaust gases are ejected downward, it will lift the aircraft vertically off the ground, provided its loaded weight is less than 5,000 lb. In the case of the 'Flying Bedstead', the exhaust of two Nene turbojets was directed downward,

and the aircraft was kept on an even keel by four downward-pointing compressed-air nozzles at the end of long arms. If its front end began to drop, more air was blown out of the forward nozzle to correct the instability—and so on.

Although the 'Flying Bedstead' looked more like a huge metal spider than an aircraft, it worked surprisingly well. Before long, the Short company had built a small delta-wing research aircraft using the same 'jet-lift' principle, proving that vertical take-off could be combined with higher forward speeds. Simultaneously, the Bristol Siddeley engine company evolved a variation of the 'jet-lift' technique, known as vectored thrust. In this, the jet exhaust is ejected through four rotating nozzles. When the nozzles are directed downward, the aircraft to which the engine is fitted is raised vertically off the ground. When it reaches a safe height, the nozzles are rotated slightly rearward, causing the aircraft to accelerate forward. When it has reached a high enough speed for the wings to support it, the nozzles are turned fully rearward so that all the engine's thrust is used for propulsion.

By using the vectored-thrust idea in its remarkable little Harrier fighter-bomber, Hawker Siddeley have been able to give the R.A.F. the first combat aircraft able to take off anywhere, carrying a heavy load of attack weapons, and dive at supersonic speed.

In the early days of powered flight, the great American inventor, Thomas Alva Edison said: 'The aeroplane won't amount to a thing until they get a machine that will act like a humming bird—go straight up, go forward, go backward, come straight down and alight like a humming bird. It isn't easy. I worked at it once, but got busy with something else. Somebody is going to do it.' Somebody has!

WINGS TO LIFT A WORLD

War kills machines as well as men. The big metal-framed airship died in World War I, when it was no longer able to live in the same sky as the nimble fighter-plane. A few were built in the 1920s and '30s; the German *Graf Zeppelin* and *Hindenburg* even pioneered transatlantic passenger travel at a time when no transport aeroplane could yet tackle such services; but by 1938 they had all disappeared. In the same way, World War 2 killed the flying-boat.

Pre-war, the four-engined flying-boat had been queen of the skies. Imperial Airways' fleet of Short 'C'-class 'boats carried passengers from Britain to every corner of the Empire, except across the Atlantic to Canada—and even made experimental flights on that route. They carried vast quantities of mail, to such a degree that all first-class mail between Britain and its Empire went by air, at the rate of only 1½ d per half-ounce—a twelfth of what it costs today to many places.

Yet, within five years and three months of the end of World War 2, Imperial Airways' successor, B.O.A.C., had operated its last flying-boat service. Again, a few 'boats have lingered on in airline use in various parts of the world; but the landplane is now unchallenged on the main international routes. The reason is easy to find.

To meet air force demands in 1939-45, aerodromes were built in every corner of the earth. Very different from the pre-war grass airports, they were provided with long concrete or tarmac runways. Later, as radio and radar navigation aids were perfected, to enable bombers to find and destroy their targets by day or night in all weathers, these aids were adapted to guide transport aircraft between airfields. Even fog and low cloud lost a little of their terror when pilots could be guided down to a safe landing by a controller on the ground, who could pinpoint the aircraft's constantly-changing position on his radar screen.

In some theatres of war, like Burma, whole armies were kept in action by dropping food, ammunition and equipment from an armada of transport aircraft. Other transports shuttled men and freight from one combat area to another in a matter of hours, compared with days by boat. More than 10,000 military versions of the DC-3 were built for this

work, followed by the four-engined C-54 (DC-4) Skymaster and Constellation, and other equally fine modern transports. When the war ended, these were released in vast numbers for use by any airline that wanted them.

With such aircraft available at knock-down prices, and plenty of aerodromes from which to operate them, airlines were no longer interested in flying-boats. The new navigation aids, which promised to make air travel far safer, were installed at land airfields; and although most places charged a sizeable landing fee for every machine using their airport, this still worked out cheaper for an airline than having to provide fire-boats, passenger-boats, maintenance services, flare-paths and all the other paraphernalia needed at a water base.

It was clear even in 1946 that there was going to be a tremendous boom in air travel. So many service-men had flown during the war that the old fear of flying had almost disappeared. People wanted to see more of the world and to spend their holidays in sunny places, and the new aircraft made this possible at the kind of fares they could afford. Even transatlantic services presented no problems, as aeroplanes had been ferried across the Atlantic as routine for years.

The American aircraft industry had good reason to face the future with confidence. It had grown rapidly in size and wealth in 1938-40 when Britain and France had placed huge orders in the United States in an effort to re-equip their air forces for the coming war. When America, too, was at war, the demand for aircraft was so great that by December 1943 production had reached a rate of 105,000 aeroplanes per year—or one every five minutes of the day and night, every day.

Britain's smaller industry also achieved miracles of production, but with one important difference. By arrangement with the U.S. government, it concentrated on turning out combat machines, leaving America to supply virtually all of the transport aircraft needed by the Allied air forces. With a war to be won, this was common-sense; but when the fighting was over, Britain realised it could not hope to match for years, if ever, America's already established

Before the war, flying-boats like the Short 'C' class, operated by Imperial Airways and Qantas, were the queens of the sky. In 1939-45, bases were built all over the world for the thousands of bombers, *opposite, top*, put into service by the Allies. In addition, landplane transports were put into large-scale production to supply the needs of the Allied armies. Post-war airlines were able to buy ex-military landplane transports cheaply and to use the new bases; and the flying-boat gradually disappeared from the major international routes.

By taking advantage of its wartime leadership in jet propulsion, Britain became the first country in the world to offer passengers the speed and comfort of jet travel, when B.O.A.C. introduced the de Havilland Comet, *opposite, bottom*, on to its London-Johannesburg route in 1952.

position in the design of piston-engined airliners.

While airlines everywhere bought American, B.O.A.C. and its new partner on European routes, B.E.A., made do with transport versions of wartime bombers, like the York, and stop-gap airliners such as the Viking and Hermes. Behind the scenes British designers planned one of the boldest advances ever made in aviation history, by taking advantage of their lead in jet-propulsion to produce the world's first jet and turboprop airliners.

This did not involve merely fitting the new-type engines to the usual type of airframe. Jets are most efficient at very high altitudes, so, in designing their Comet jet-liner, de Havilland had to make it suitable for operation at up to 40,000 ft. This meant that the fuselage had to be pressurised — pumped full of air to enable passengers and crew to breathe normally in the rarefied atmosphere seven miles above the earth. Pressurisation was not new. Boeing had built a lightly-pressurised airliner before the war; but the Comet had to be built strongly enough to withstand a pressure of $8\frac{1}{4}$ lb. on every square inch of its cabin walls, trying to burst them outward.

In exchange for all the problems, both known and unknown, the Comet promised to give passengers the fastest, smoothest air travel they had ever known. Its cabin was to be fully air-conditioned, and a cruising height of more than 30,000 ft. would clearly put it above most of the bad

weather through which unpressurised piston-engined aircraft often had to battle.

The gamble very nearly came off. Even when it entered scheduled service with B.O.A.C. on May 2, 1952, no other company in the world had a jet airliner in production. Airlines in France, Canada, Australia, Venezuela, Japan and Brazil, and even the great Pan American World Airways, placed orders for the Comet, realising that passengers would quickly learn to prefer its unrivalled speed and comfort, to the detriment of airlines flying the piston-engined machines that were already beginning to look old-fashioned.

Unfortunately, Britain was to pay a high price for its pioneering. On January 10, 1954, a B.O.A.C. Comet broke up in the air over Elba, for no apparent reason, soon after taking off for Rome. A little earlier, another Comet had disintegrated near Calcutta, but as it had been flying through a tropical storm at the time no fault in the aircraft had been suspected. This time it was different. The Comet was grounded, but still nobody could find anything wrong with its design or construction. The end came on April 8, 1954 when, a fortnight after re-entering service, a South African Airways Comet disappeared in similar circumstances off the coast of Sicily. The Comet was again grounded—this time for keeps.

With great skill, using every modern technique, including underwater television, the Royal Navy managed to salvage

Almost everything that can be got inside a transport aircraft, whole or in sections, has been carried by air at some time or other. Typical air cargoes are shown below. The Brantly helicopter, *top left*, has too short a range to fly the Atlantic itself, so it travels inside a B.O.A.C. freighter. The lessened possibility of damage, compared with surface transport, eliminates the need for crates and reduces en route insurance costs. Precious objects like the silver casks, *top right*, containing parchment scrolls on which are handwritten, in old Hebrew, five books of Moses, also travel more safely by air and take up little room on the aircraft. Animal travellers sometimes outnumber humans, and a favourite passenger on B.E.A's London-Moscow service in 1966 was London Zoo's panda Chi-Chi.

To speed the loading and unloading of bulky freight, many transport aircraft have large nose or tail loading doors, and cabin floors which are the same height above the ground as the bed of a lorry. B.E.A's Argosies, *top*, have doors at both the front and the rear of their cargo-hold. Freight, pre-loaded on pallets, is moved easily on roller-conveyors built into the floor of the cabin and the bed of the lorries. Russia's Mil Mi-6 helicopter, *bottom*, is also large enough to carry motor cars, which are loaded by driving up a ramp between the clamshell rear doors of the hold. Alternative loads include 65 passengers. The Mi-6 cruises at 155 m.p.h. and is fitted with small fixed wings which reduce the loading on the rotor in flight. Fuel is carried in tanks strapped on to each side of the cabin.

Recent years have seen a tremendous growth in private and club flying and in what is called general aviation. This term covers all commercial activities other than those conducted by airlines, and includes crop-spraying and dusting, air taxi services, aerial surveying and ambulance work.

Even small four-seat lightplanes like the French 150-h.p. Morane-Saulnier Super Rallye can accomodate a stretcher. Their speed, allied to the fact that they can operate from shorter runways than the usual, larger, air ambulances, has saved many lives.

The American Cessna company alone manufactures more than 6,500 private and business aircraft each year. The bottom left picture on this page shows batches of Cessna two-seat and four-seat lightplanes awaiting delivery.

Typical of specialised aerobatic-training and championship-flying aircraft—the Czech Zlin 526 Trener-Master, *bottom right*. Both single- and two-seater versions are powered by a 160-h.p. Walter Minor 6-111 piston-engine. Fuel and oil systems keep the engine working during 4 minutes' inverted flight.

More than 2,000 Cessna 150 lightplanes, *top left*, are built annually. Powered by a 100-h.p. Continental piston-engine, the 150 carries two adults and two children 565 miles at 93 m.p.h. Its maximum speed is 122 m.p.h.

Larger and more unusual Cessna light aircraft is the Model 337 Super Skymaster, *top right*. It is a 'push-and-pull' twin-engined monoplane, with one 210-h.p. piston-engine in the nose and another behind the cabin, between the twin tail-booms. With this arrangement, it is much easier to keep the aircraft straight and level if one engine should fail. The Super Skymaster carries up to six persons at 141-192 m.p.h. and can be fitted with an underfuselage container for baggage or freight, as shown.

The Snow Commander agricultural aircraft, *bottom*, carries more than a ton of chemicals in a hopper forward of the cockpit. Liquids are sprayed from nozzle-bars along the wing trailing-edges. Dusts are spread from a gate beneath the hopper, as illustrated. This is dangerous work in rough country and calls for skilled piloting and a highly manoeuvrable and sturdy aircraft.

SHAPES OF THE SIXTIES Two basic vertical take-off and landing (VTOL) jet-lift techniques are being used in 'next-generation' combat aircraft. One is the vectored-thrust method employed in the Hawker Siddeley Harrier, see page 114, in which a single engine with rotating nozzles is used for both lift and propulsion. The alternative method, used in the French Dassault Mirage III-V experimental VTOL fighter prototypes, *below*, has separate engines for lift and propulsion.

Four pairs of Rolls-Royce RB.162 lift-jets, mounted vertically under the air-intake doors shown open in the picture, raised the Mirage III-V off the ground. At a safe height, the main SNECMA TF-106 jet-engine, mounted horizontally in the rear fuselage, was opened up to propel the aircraft forward. When speed was sufficiently high for the wings to provide adequate lift, the lift-jets were switched off and the intake doors closed.

Twin tail-booms are a characteristic of many aircraft designed for freight carrying. Their use enables vehicles to drive right up to the doors which form the rear of the fuselage, for direct loading into the freight-hold. The twin-boomed Hawker Siddeley Argosy, *top*, is powered by four 2,230-h.p. Rolls-Royce Dart turboprops and can carry 14½ tons of cargo 485 miles at a cruising speed of 280 m.p.h.

Pointer to the future is the American LTV XC-142A, *bottom*, of which five prototypes were built for testing by the U.S. Services. It is a tilt-wing aircraft, powered by four 2,850-h.p. General Electric T64 turboprops and able to carry 32 troops or 3½ tons of freight. Top speed is 431 m.p.h. By tilting the wing through 90 degrees, so that the propellers work as helicopter rotors, the pilot is able to take off and land vertically. A small rotor at the tail helps to keep the aircraft on an even keel at this stage. Once off the ground, the pilot tilts the wing forward slightly, so that the propellers provide both lift and propulsion.

Largest jet airliner in the late '60s, the Douglas DC-8 Super 63, *top*, is a 'stretched' version of the original DC-8 able to carry up to 259 passengers at 600 m.p.h. Such aircraft cost well over £3 million each, but can carry more passengers over the Atlantic in a year than an ocean liner the size of the *Queen Mary*.

The lower illustration on this page shows the famous French Caravelle — the airliner which set a completely new fashion

by carrying its two Rolls-Royce Avon jet-engines on the sides of the rear fuselage. This not only improved the efficiency of the wings, by leaving them free of engine pods or air intakes, but also made the Caravelle the quietest airliner in the world, so far as its passengers were concerned, when it entered service in mid-1959. Eighty passengers can be carried at speeds up to 525 m.p.h.

the remains of the Elba Comet. There followed an investigation as detailed and enthralling as anything in a 'whodunnit'. The remains of the Comet were pieced together at the Royal Aircraft Establishment, Farnborough, and after months of work the cause of the disasters was clear. Repeated pressurising of the fuselage after take-off, and de-pressurising before landing, had weakened the fuselage, which had simply burst under the strain. 'Metal fatigue' became the new public enemy No. 1 of the jet-age aircraft designer, and has remained so ever since.

Every aircraft manufacturer in the world profited from de Havilland's hard-earned experience, and admitted this. Strengthened, lengthened and re-designed as the Comet 4, Britain's pioneer jet-liner went on to achieve the success it deserved, enabling B.O.A.C. to become the first airline able to offer a transatlantic jet service, on October 4, 1958. But other countries had not wasted the four lost years. Russia's national airline, Aeroflot, had entered the jet age two years earlier, in September 1956, and Boeing 707 and Douglas DC-8 jet-liners were rolling along vast assembly lines in America, to challenge and eclipse Britain's achievement. Only in turboprop travel was Britain still the undisputed leader, for the Viscount was in a class by itself on short-range and medium-range services and more than 400 were eventually sold.

Air travel grew at a fantastic rate. Before long more people were crossing the Atlantic by air than by ship, and the total number of air travellers became astronomical. In 1945, about 9,000,000 flew on scheduled airline services all over the world, excluding Russia and China which published no figures. The total 24 years later had risen to nearly 290,000,000, of whom more than 5,250,000 flew over the Atlantic.

Yet this represents only part of the story of modern air transport, for the growth of air freighting has been equally impressive. At one time, the only goods worth air freighting were the precious and perishable. Nothing is more out-of-date than yesterday's news so, long before World War II Imperial Airways operated nightly 'newspaper specials' between London and Paris. Freshly-cut flowers and day-old chicks appeared often on the cargo list. So did diamonds, bank-notes and bullion, which were far safer in an airliner in flight than they would have been on a boat or train.

The advent of specially-designed cargo-planes like the Bristol Freighter, with big nose or tail loading doors, opened up tremendous new possibilities after the war. It was found that animals such as race-horses were far less nervous and tired after flying than after a boat journey. Even furniture could be carried across the English Channel more cheaply by air, if one offset against the higher freight charge the reduced insurance rate and the fact that much less expensive packing was needed.

Most surprising of all was the success of the cross-Channel

World's most popular airliner, because of its speed, comfort and safety, the British Aircraft Corporation's Super VC10, *top right*, entered service on BOAC's trans-Atlantic route on April 1, 1965. Four Rolls-Royce Conway engines, each giving 22,500 lb. of thrust, enable it to carry up to 174 passengers at 568 m.p.h., but the BOAC version is fitted out to carry 16 first class and 123 economy class passengers in rather more spacious seating.

Germany's little HFB 320 Hansa business jet, *lower picture*, combines rear-mounted engines with unique swept-forward wings, which give the passengers an unusually good downward view in flight, as they are mounted behind the cabin. Up to nine passengers are normally carried, and the Hansa cruises at 420-513 m.p.h.

FROM THE SUBLIME... The three-jet Boeing 727 airliner, seen cruising over Mount Rainier in the large picture on the right, might be termed sublime, but the little single-seat Tempête sporting aircraft, *top left*, are far from ridiculous. Built at home, by do-it-yourself constructor-pilots, they can fly at 120 m.p.h. on only 65 h.p. and cost a few hundred pounds to make. The airframe is entirely of wood.

The average amateur constructor takes about two years to build an aeroplane like the Tempête in his spare time. By comparison, some hundreds of thousands of man-hours go into the construction of a large four-jet airliner. This helps to explain why the Boeing Company needs more than 100,000 employees to keep pace with orders for its Boeing 707, *bottom left*, and other jet-liners, as well as its military contracts.

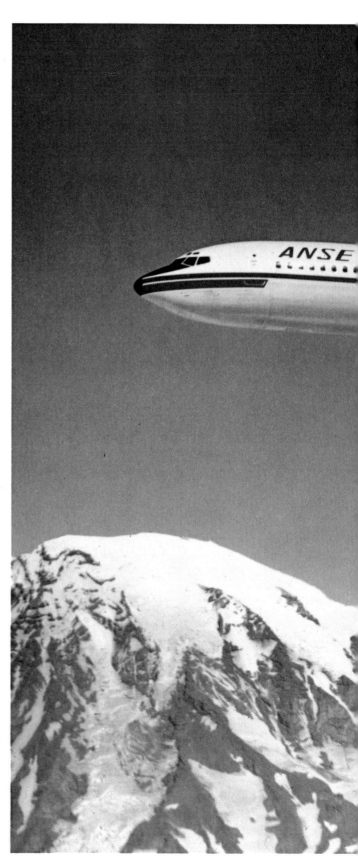

In its original form, the American Boeing supersonic airliner had a swing-wing, with the four engines mounted under the tailplane. This was changed in 1968-9 for a more conventional design, the delta-wing Model 2707-300, with the engines in underwing pods. To cope with the high temperatures built up by air friction at its cruising speed of 1,800 m.p.h., this big 283-ton aircraft will be built of heat-resistant metals such as titanium and stainless steel. The cabin will accommodate 250-321 passengers, and it is hoped to have the 2707-300 in service by 1978.

According to Douglas Aircraft engineers, even 1,800-m.p.h. supersonic airliners may seem slow by the end of the 20th century. They believe that by then it will be possible to send up to 170 passengers at a time to the other side of the Earth in just 45 minutes by using giant rocket-liners of the kind shown below. They claim it would be safer and more comfortable than even present-day jet travel — only the potential passengers remain to be convinced!

car ferry service started by Silver City Airways in 1948. Fares, inevitably, were higher than by boat, but were reduced year by year as business grew. Soon tens of thousands of people were flying with their cars each year and Silver City's Bristol Freighters were taking off and landing at 3½-minute intervals in daylight hours on peak days.

Today, even four-engined jets are used for freighting and it is safe to say that anything which can be packed into an aeroplane, either whole or in pieces, must have been carried by air at some time or other.

The growth in business has had to be matched by a corresponding increase in the size of transport aircraft. A DC-3 of 1947 carried 28 passengers. Its modern successor, the mighty Boeing 747 'jumbo-jet', has seats for up to four hundred and ninety passengers in cabins more than twenty feet wide. Cruising speeds have increased just as dramatically, from the DC-3's 185 m.p.h. to the 747's 580 m.p.h. which will be more than doubled when the 1,400 m.p.h. Anglo-French Concorde supersonic airliner enters service in the early 1970s.

The Concorde offers proof that Europe's aircraft industry can still lead the world, for it is years ahead of its larger American competitor.

Increasing speeds have brought changing shapes to air travel, from the straight wings of wartime transports to the sweptback wings of the Comet and the delta wing of the Concorde. The Caravelle introduced the new fashion of having its jet-engines mounted on the sides of the rear fuselage. Every different idea has its advantages and disadvantages; the job of the designer is to give his aircraft as many as possible of the advantages, without too many

of the disadvantages. The trouble is that, for example, the sweptback wing, which is ideal for high-speed cruising, is not nearly as good as a straight wing at low speeds. If only wings could change shape in flight... and why not? The Germans first considered doing this on a Messerschmitt fighter during the war. The Americans tried it out on the Bell X-5 research aircraft in the early 1950s and are now using the 'swing-wing' on their F-111 fighter-bomber, enabling it to land and take off comparatively slowly with the wings forward and to cruise at 2½ times the speed of sound with them swept back.

This is only one of a number of advanced ideas that will enable us to fly faster, more safely, at less cost and in greater comfort in the years ahead. Most improvements in airliner design have been tried out first in military aircraft through the years, and it may not be long before supersonic airliners inherit vertical take-off ability from the Harrier. Already they are getting to the stage of landing under automatic control in fog and bad weather—a new technique developed for use by Britain's jet-bombers, and adopted eagerly by the airlines.

Even the guided missile may contribute something to future air travel, for Douglas designers have suggested packing passengers, 170 at a time, into a huge rocket that would carry them from Los Angeles to Honolulu in 18 minutes or to the most distant point on the globe in just 45 minutes. This may sound a little frightening—but our present 600-m.p.h. jet-liners, flying seven miles up, under automatic control, would probably have seemed just as alarming to the little group of Life Guards who watched Orville Wright make his 120-ft. switchback flight in 1903.

WINGS TO LIFT A WORLD One way to enable passengers to travel faster, in more comfort and at less expense, is to cut down to as little as 40 minutes the time spent by airliners on the ground between flights. Some of the ground equipment needed to service a Super VC10 is shown here in the upper illustration.

A major problem is to ensure that time saved in the air is not wasted on the ground at airports. To speed loading and unloading of freight, the Canadair Forty-Four, *lower picture*, has a swing-tail, so that cargoes can be transferred straight from trucks into the huge hold.

The pictures on the opposite page depict two of the aircraft that are revolutionising air travel in the 'seventies. The Boeing 747 'jumbo-jet', *top*, can carry up to 490 passengers, ten-abreast, in a cabin 20 ft. wide; but the first examples to enter service are equipped to seat only some 360 people. The resulting standard of comfort is extremely high. The Anglo-French Concorde, *lower picture*, will carry 128-144 passengers when it enters service in 1973 and will link London with New York in about 3 hours.

OUT INTO SPACE

'The next war', said the late Colonel-General Baron von Fritsch in 1939, just before it started, 'will be won by the military organisation with the most efficient photographic reconnaissance.' He was right; it was. But reconnaissance can also prevent wars. That is why another military leader, General Eisenhower, proposed during the period when he was President of the United States that his country and Russia should sign an 'Open Skies' agreement. Under this, each nation would have been entitled to fly over the other's territory, keeping track of military installations such as rocket sites and ensuring that no preparations for war could be made secretly.

America had proof of the value of such flights. For some time it had been sending high-flying Lockheed U-2 spy-planes over Russia to photograph places of interest. At first, these machines were either undetected or beyond the range of Soviet interceptor fighters and missiles. Then, on May 1, 1960, a U-2 piloted by Francis Gary Powers was brought down near Sverdlovsk, deep inside Russia, and the whole world learned of the desperate lengths to which America was prepared to go to reduce the danger of a surprise attack on her territory or that of her friends.

President Eisenhower said that there would be no more flights over the Soviet Union, but this seems to have excluded Russia's satellites and allies. On October 16, 1962, his successor, President Kennedy, was shown photographs, taken by U.S. reconnaissance aircraft, of Soviet medium-range war rockets that were being installed in Cuba. Clearly, these posed a direct threat to America, as much of its territory was within range of the missiles. The President warned Cuba that they must be sent back to Russia or he would be compelled to take appropriate action. For a time, it seemed that the world was at the very brink of a nuclear war; then Soviet Prime Minister Krushchev agreed to remove the missiles if America would call off her blockade of Cuba and promise not to invade it. The crisis was over and the value of reconnaissance had been proved again.

Today most aerial reconnaissance is done by flying around the borders of other countries, without infringing their sovereignty. Much can be learned this way, by long-range

Military reconnaissance aircraft have come a long way since they first proved their worth in the 1914-18 War. A 'spy-plane' that hit the headlines in 1960, when one was shot down over Russia, was the Lockheed U-2, *top left.* Another American photo reconnaissance aircraft that achieved considerable success was the LTV RF-8A Crusader, *centre.* Flying from U.S. Navy carriers, it discovered Soviet long-range missiles in Cuba in 1962, provoking an international incident which led to removal of the rockets. The Boeing Stratotanker, *bottom*, bristles with aerials for electronic equipment used to keep a check on other nations' installations.

Designed as a successor to the U-2, the Lockheed SR-71A strategic reconnaissance aircraft *top* is the first operational type able to cruise at more than 2,000 m.p.h. at great heights. As well as cameras, it carries electronic apparatus for monitoring radio and radar installations.

A more conventional reconnaissance aircraft is the Swedish Saab S 35E Draken, *bottom*, shown here with the seven cameras which it is able to carry in its nose.

A new era of human exploration and adventure opened on April 12, 1961, when Yuri Gagarin of Russia became the first man to orbit the Earth in the spacecraft *Vostok 1* (*below, top*). Launched by a multi-stage rocket, *bottom left*, the spacecraft consisted of a spherical man-carrying capsule attached to a cylindrical instrument section housing the *Vostok*'s steering rockets, oxygen containers, electrical power supply units, radio, TV equipment and the retro-rockets used to slow the craft so that the capsule could be released for re-entry into the atmosphere.

When American astronauts Borman and Lovell boarded their Gemini 7 spacecraft, *bottom right*, they wore suits with specially-large helmets to provide extra comfort during their record 14 days in orbit.

Bell's lunar flying vehicle, *opposite page, top*, was designed as a runabout for astronauts exploring the Moon. For the return journey from orbiting space stations of the future, ferry craft very like the Northrop HL-10 wingless research vehicle, *opposite, bottom*, will probably be used.

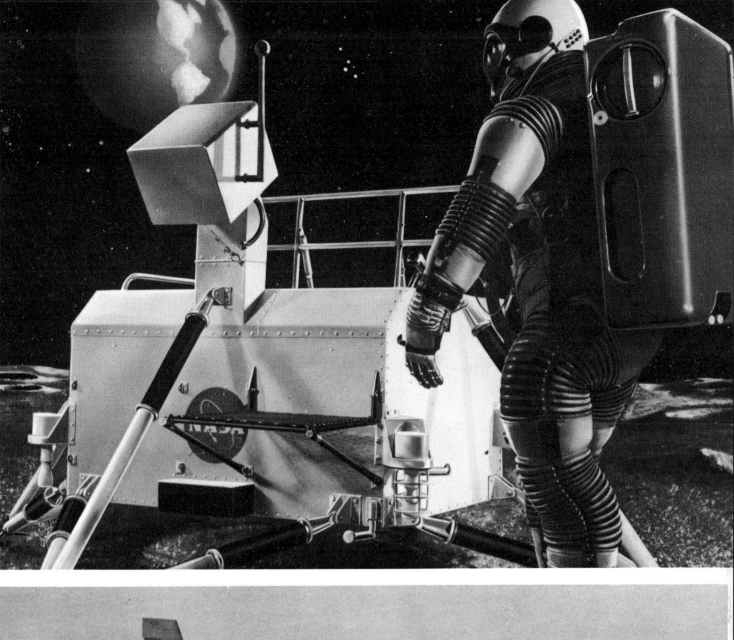

The ability to rendezvous at will with other spacecraft in orbit was an essential preliminary to exploration of the Moon and the establishment of large space stations in orbit around the Earth. On December 15, 1965, a manned spacecraft made such a rendezvous with another for the first time. This remarkable photograph, taken 160 miles above the Earth, shows the Gemini 7 spacecraft of astronauts Borman and Lovell as it appeared from the hatchway of Gemini 6, during the period when the two craft orbited together at more than 15,000 m.p.h.

photography and by 'listening' to radio and radar signals to discover how advanced is the equipment in use by the nation under surveillance. But more and more of the work is being taken over by satellites, which can fly repeatedly over any place on earth without attracting complaints, as no-one has yet decided whether space flights of any kind can be declared illegal.

How good are the photographs taken by satellites? The best clue was given by Mr Krushchev's son-in-law, who said that pictures brought back by U.S. satellites were so clear that the name on the *Pravda* newspaper offices in Moscow could be read. Nor should we imagine that objects put into orbit will remain purely defensive, for the Russians already have an FOBS missile (see page 108) which can put an H-bomb warhead into Earth orbit.

So, already, space flight is being used for military purposes, just as the aeroplane learned to kill before it became really useful for anything else. There could be no sadder commentary on man's mentality, for here is one branch of science in which all nations should be working together.

Even working individually, Russia and America have made fantastic progress in the 13 years since the first little satellite, *Sputnik 1*, bleeped its way around the earth on October 4, 1957. Well over 1,000 satellites have followed in its wake, telling us much about the world in which we live and the space around it, teaching us about our weather by means of meteorological reports from space, passing television pictures halfway across the world so that we can see events almost everywhere as they happen, offering more accurate navigation, better long-distance telephone services and a host of other benefits.

Less than ten years have passed since Yuri Gagarin became the first man to orbit the earth in *Vostok 1*, on April 12, 1961. Yet such journeys have become so routine that few people could name all of the Soviet and American astronauts who have followed him. Some have stepped outside the cramped cabins of their craft to 'walk' in space, as they hurtled at 17,000 m.p.h., more than 100 miles above our heads. They have seen wonders that are hidden from our eyes, and have even walked the surface of another world by voyaging 250,000 miles through space to the Moon.

Of course, this is not flying, although the shape of *Vostok 1* is very like the sphere in which Cyrano de Bergerac's fictional hero rose towards the Moon by 'dew-power', at a time when men were still jumping off towers with flapping wings. So much has happened in so tiny a span of history that we may, perhaps, have forgotten what it was that men once dreamed of doing. When the real flyers, the birds, look down at 200,000,000 people crawling into metal cylinders with wings—like pieces of toothpaste in a tube—while other men are sealed into tiny capsules and shot into space, returning like fireballs, they may consider it all rather a joke.

Apollo II spacecraft being lifted off the launch pad at Cape Kennedy by its Saturn V rocket on July 16, 1969. The complete vehicle was 353 ft. 5 in. high.

Aldrin stepping down the *Eagle*'s ladder on to the surface of the Moon on July 20. This photograph was taken by Armstrong—the first man ever to set foot on the Moon.

When the spacecraft entered orbit around the Moon, the Lunar Module *Eagle* was detached from the nose of the Command Module, to carry astronauts Neil Armstrong and Edwin Aldrin down to the lunar surface. It is here seen returning.

INDEX

ACKNOWLEDGEMENTS

The Aeroplane
Air B. P.
Robert D. Archer
Spencer Arnold
Automotor Journal
Association des Amis du Musée de l'Air
Author's Collection
Avions Marcel Dassault
Bell Aerosystems Company
B.O.A.C.
Boeing Aircraft Company
The British Aircraft Company
British European Airways
The British Petroleum Company Ltd
Charles E. Brown
Canadair
Central Office of Information, Crown Copyright
  reserved
Central Press Photos Ltd
De Havilland Aircraft Co. Ltd
Douglas Aircraft Company
Eastern Airlines
Joe Fallon
Flight
General Dynamics Corporation
Gloster Aircraft Co. Ltd
Hamburger Flugzeugbau GMBH
Akira Hasegawa
Hawker Siddeley Aviation
I.C.I. Ltd
Illustrations Bureau
Imperial War Museum
Marcel Jurca
A. T. Kelly & Co. Ltd

Keystone Press Agency Ltd
Koston Studio
Howard Levy
The Library of Congress
Ling-Tenco-Vaught Inc.
Lockheed Aircraft Corporation
London Express Pictures
Karel Masojidek
Harry McDougall
MoD., Crown Copyright reserved
Musée des Arts et Métiers Collection
N.A.S.A.
North American Aviation Inc.
Novosti Press Agency
Stephen P. Peltz
Press Association Photos Ltd
Pressed Steel Company
Qantas
R.A.A.F.
Radio Times Hulton Picture Library
A.V. Roe & Co. Ltd
Rolls Royce Ltd
The Science Museum
Sikorsky Aircraft
Smithsonian Institution
Alex Stöcker
I. Thuresson
Twentieth Century Fox
U.S. Air Force
U.S. Information Service
U.S. Navy
L. Vallin Collection
Gordon S. Williams